Exploring land use impact on conservation efforts

Exploring land use impact on conservation efforts

Sanyub S.

UNIEK ENTERPRISES

CONTENTS

Introduction

INTRODUCTION

The complex connection between land use and protection endeavors has turned into a fundamental worry notwithstanding raising ecological difficulties and the critical requirement for reasonable turn of events. As human populaces prosper and worldwide requests for assets increase, the manner in which we use and oversee land has significant ramifications for biodiversity, environments, and the general strength of our planet. This investigation dives into the multi-layered elements of land use and its effect on protection, meaning to disclose the intricacies, difficulties, and amazing open doors that lie at the crossing point of human turn of events and natural conservation.

Contextualizing Area Use and Preservation:

Land use, in the broadest sense, envelops the different manners by which land is used by human social orders. This incorporates private, modern, agrarian, and sporting purposes, among others. Protection, then again, is the purposeful work to defend and reasonably oversee regular assets, environments, and biodiversity. The crossing point of these two domains turns out to be especially basic as anthropogenic exercises progressively infringe upon normal territories, frequently prompting environment annihilation, fracture, and loss of biodiversity.

Authentic Points of view Ashore Use and Protection:

To comprehend the ongoing elements of land use and protection, following the verifiable advancement of human communications with the environment is fundamental. Conventional social orders frequently had cooperative associations with nature, depending on manageable practices that kept a sensitive harmony between asset use and safeguarding. Be that as it may, with the coming of industrialization and modernization, the interest for land and assets flooded, prompting far and wide deforestation, natural surroundings obliteration, and overexploitation.

The development of the protection development in the late nineteenth and mid twentieth hundreds of years denoted a defining moment. Visionaries like John Muir and Theodore Roosevelt supported for the protection of wild regions and the foundation of public parks, laying the preparation for current preservation standards. As social orders wrestled with the natural outcomes of uncontrolled turn of events, a worldwide consciousness of the requirement for supportable land use rehearses started to flourish.

Contemporary Difficulties in Land Use and Preservation:

In the 21st 100 years, the nexus between land use and preservation faces exceptional difficulties. Fast urbanization, agrarian extension, and infrastructural improvement apply gigantic strain on regular biological systems.

The transformation of backwoods into farming terrains, the multiplication of endless suburbia, and the extraction of normal assets for financial increase add to living space misfortune and discontinuity, representing an immediate danger to various plant and animal species.

Environmental change further intensifies these difficulties, adjusting scenes and affecting the dispersion of species. Increasing temperatures, changing precipitation examples, and outrageous climate occasions can upset biological systems and challenge the capacity of species to adjust. The fragile equilibrium that supports biodiversity is under danger, requiring a reexamination of land use practices to relieve the effect on protection endeavors.

Biodiversity Areas of interest and Land Use Increase:

Certain districts all over the planet are perceived as biodiversity areas of interest, holding onto an excessively big number of species, a considerable lot of which are endemic and indispensable. Tragically, these regions are much of the time ideal objectives for serious land use exercises. Horticulture, logging, and foundation improvement can quickly change these areas of interest, prompting the deficiency of novel species and biological capabilities.

Endeavors to escalate land use for expanded farming creation, driven by the developing worldwide populace, represent a huge test to preservation. The development of monoculture crops, the utilization of agrochemicals, and the transformation of assorted scenes into homogenous agrarian fields can bring about the exhaustion of soil fruitfulness, water contamination, and the downfall of pollinator populaces — all of which have flowing impacts on biodiversity.

The Job of Urbanization in Land Use and Preservation:

Urbanization is an inescapable worldwide pattern with significant ramifications for land use and protection. As metropolitan regions grow, they frequently consume immense parcels of land, dividing normal territories and secluding populaces of plants and creatures. Endless suburbia changes scenes as well as presents contamination, obtrusive species, and fake light, further testing the flexibility of environments.

Nonetheless, urban areas likewise present special open doors for preservation endeavors. Practical metropolitan preparation, green framework, and the consolidation of green spaces inside metropolitan conditions can add to biodiversity preservation. Metropolitan protection drives look to work out some kind of harmony between human turn of events and biological safeguarding, recognizing the interconnectedness of metropolitan and normal environments.

Native Information and Conventional Land Use:

Native people group, with their profound association with the land, have for quite some time been stewards of biodiversity. Conventional land use rehearses frequently include an all encompassing comprehension of biological systems, stressing reasonable asset the executives and the conservation of biodiversity. Native information frameworks offer significant experiences into agreeable conjunction with nature, testing traditional thoughts of land utilize that focus on monetary addition over environmental respectability.

Perceiving the freedoms and information on native people groups is indispensable to compelling protection methodologies. Cooperative endeavors that include native networks in dynamic cycles can prompt more supportable land use rehearses that regard social variety and add to the protection of biodiversity.

Mechanical Developments and Land Use Arranging:

In the journey for feasible land use, innovation assumes a significant part. Remote detecting, geographic data frameworks (GIS), and other cutting edge innovations empower exact planning and checking of land cover changes. These apparatuses engage land use organizers, policymakers, and traditionalists to go with informed choices, distinguish need regions for preservation, and evaluate the viability of protection measures.

Additionally, arising advancements, for example, accuracy horticulture and reasonable ranger service rehearses offer answers for accommodate human necessities with natural assurance. Accuracy farming, for example, utilizes information driven ways to deal with upgrade asset use, limit ecological effect, and improve horticultural efficiency. Coordinating mechanical advancements into land use arranging can prepare for more practical and environmentally sound turn of events.

Legitimate and Strategy Structures for Reasonable Land Use:

The detailing and requirement of hearty legitimate and strategy systems are instrumental in molding land use rehearses that line up with protection objectives. Legislatures, worldwide associations, and nearby networks should team up to lay out guidelines that focus on ecological supportability, biodiversity preservation, and the impartial circulation of assets.

Safeguarded regions, untamed life passageways, and cradle zones are instances of land use assignments expected to defend basic environments and advance availability between biological systems. Compelling implementation of these assignments requires a blend of legitimate instruments, local area commitment, and global collaboration to address transboundary preservation challenges.

Monetary Contemplations and Preservation:

One of the perpetual difficulties in the crossing point of land use and protection is the strain between financial turn of events and biological safeguarding. Many land use choices are driven by financial contemplations, frequently leaning toward momentary increases over long haul maintainability. Offsetting financial improvement with preservation requires a change in perspective in the manner we esteem environments and regular assets.

The idea of biological system administrations highlights the innate worth of nature in supporting human prosperity. By perceiving the heap benefits given by environments — like clean water, fertilization, and environment guideline — monetary models can be adjusted to represent the genuine expense of impractical land use rehearses. Coordinating financial motivations for preservation can adjust the interests of partners and cultivate a more amicable connection between land use and protection.

Worldwide Joint effort for Worldwide Protection:

Given the interconnected idea of biological systems and the cross-line development of species, global coordinated effort is basic for powerful preservation. Worldwide drives, like the Show on Organic Variety (CBD), expect to cultivate collaboration among countries to address the deficiency of biodiversity and advance maintainable land use rehearses.

Peaceful accords give a system to sharing information, assets, and innovations to handle normal protection challenges. Be that as it may, difficulties like lopsided execution, absence of implementation systems, and varying needs among countries feature the intricacy of accomplishing worldwide protection objectives. Reinforcing global collaboration and cultivating a common feeling of obligation are fundamental for tending to land use influences on a planetary scale.

Contextual analyses: Gaining from Progress and Disappointment:

Inspecting contextual analyses from different locales offers important bits of knowledge into the perplexing interaction between land use and preservation. Examples of overcoming adversity, like the recuperation of specific jeopardized species or the rebuilding of debased scenes, give motivation and significant illustrations to future preservation endeavors. On the other hand, occasions of disappointment and potentially negative results highlight the requirement for versatile administration and a nuanced comprehension of neighborhood settings.

Contextual analyses might incorporate instances of feasible land use rehearses, local area drove preservation drives, or examples where financial turn of events and protection objectives have been effectively coordinated. Dissecting both positive and adverse results adds to a more far reaching comprehension of the difficulties and open doors intrinsic in the connection between land use and preservation.

Future Possibilities and Arising Difficulties:

As we explore the Anthropocene, described by phenomenal human impact in the world, the eventual fate of land use and preservation is at a junction. Arising difficulties, for example, the rising interest for assets, environmental change influences, and the potential for novel advances to reshape scenes, require ground breaking techniques. The mix of protection standards into arising fields, like practical metropolitan plan, roundabout economies, and regenerative farming, holds guarantee for a more maintainable future.

Tackling the force of development, cultivating interdisciplinary cooperation, and drawing in nearby networks in preservation endeavors are key parts of a versatile and versatile way to deal with land use. What's in store requests a comprehensive comprehension of the perplexing collaborations between human social orders and the climate, with a pledge to cultivating an agreeable concurrence that supports biodiversity and guarantees the prosperity of people in the future.

1. Definition of Land Use Change

Land use change is a dynamic and unavoidable peculiarity that assumes an essential part in forming the World's scenes and biological systems. It alludes to changes in the ways in which land is used, enveloping changes in land cover, land the executives rehearses, and the change of normal environments into anthropogenic scenes. This investigation digs into the complex elements of land use change, planning to give a complete comprehension of its definitions, drivers, and the expansive ramifications it has on the climate, society, and feasible turn of events.

Meaning of Land Use Change:

At its center, land use change includes any perceivable distinction in the reason or the board of land over the long haul. It typifies a range of exercises, going from the transformation of regular scenes to metropolitan regions or rural fields to the deserting of horticultural grounds prompting reforestation. Land use change isn't restricted to the actual adjustment of the land cover yet in addition envelops alterations in land the board rehearses, for example, changes in crop types, water system strategies, or ranger service rehearses.

Researchers and analysts utilize different wordings to depict various parts of land use change. Land use change is many times grouped into two essential classifications: transformation and escalation. Change includes a shift starting with one land use type then onto the next, like the change of woodlands into farming fields or the urbanization of country regions. Escalation, then again, alludes to the more proficient or strengthened utilization of existing area, similar to the transformation of customary horticulture to high return monoculture.

Drivers of Land Use Change:

Understanding the drivers behind land use change is fundamental for grasping the complicated transaction of variables that add to modifications in land cover and the board. These drivers are different and interconnected, mirroring the impact of social, monetary, political, and natural powers. A portion of the key drivers include:

1. **Populace Development and Urbanization:** The tenacious development of the worldwide populace and the comparing urbanization patterns apply huge

tension ashore assets. As additional individuals move to metropolitan regions, the interest for lodging, foundation, and modern spaces prompts the change of normal scenes into urbanized conditions.

2. **Horticultural Development:** The need to take care of a developing populace drives the extension of farming terrains. Woodlands, prairies, and other normal environments are frequently changed over into huge scope agrarian fields to fulfill the need for food and products. This transformation can bring about natural surroundings misfortune, soil corruption, and biodiversity decline.

3. **Foundation Improvement:** The development of streets, expressways, dams, and other framework undertakings can cause huge land use change. These tasks frequently require the getting free from land, adjusting normal environments and adding to discontinuity, which can have flowing impacts on untamed life and biodiversity.

4. **Mechanical Headways:** Advances in innovation, like enhancements in agrarian practices or changes in land the executives methods, can drive land use change. For instance, the reception of accuracy horticulture might prompt changes in crop types, water system strategies, and the general power of land use.

5. **Strategy and Administration:** Government arrangements and guidelines assume a significant part in forming land use designs. Arrangements connected with land residency, protection, and drafting can impact whether land is utilized for agribusiness, preservation, metropolitan turn of events, or different purposes.

6. **Environmental Change:** Changes in environment examples can affect land use by impacting the reasonableness of regions for specific exercises. Changes in temperature and precipitation might adjust horticultural reasonableness, influence water accessibility, and add to changes in vegetation cover.

7. **Financial Elements:** Monetary powers, for example, market interest for specific items, impact land use choices. Benefit thought processes might drive the change of regular scenes into regions more helpful for financial exercises, like horticulture or mining.

8. **Social and Social Elements:** Social practices, customs, and cultural inclinations additionally add to land use change. For example, social practices might impact the selection of harvests filled in a specific region or the administration of common terrains.

Remote Detecting and Checking Area Use Change:

The coming of remote detecting innovation has upset the capacity to screen and measure land use change for an enormous scope. Satellite symbolism, geographic data frameworks (GIS), and other remote detecting apparatuses empower specialists to follow changes in land cover with accuracy. These innovations give significant information to surveying the degree and effect of land use change, working with informed independent direction and strategy improvement.

Remote detecting takes into consideration the production of land cover maps, distinguishing proof of land use changes, and the checking of patterns over the long haul. Constant observing gives an abundance of data about the spatial examples of land use change, assisting scientists and policymakers with grasping the elements and drivers of these changes.

Ramifications of Land Use Change:

Land use change has significant ramifications for environments, biodiversity, environment, and human prosperity. The outcomes of land use change are frequently interconnected and can appear at different spatial and fleeting scales. A portion of the key ramifications include:

1. **Biodiversity Misfortune:** Environment transformation, discontinuity, and debasement coming about because of land use change are significant drivers of biodiversity misfortune. As normal scenes are changed, species might lose their natural surroundings or become confined, prompting decreases in populaces and, at times, eliminations.

2. **Environmental Change:** Land use change adds to environmental change through different components. Deforestation, for instance, discharges put away carbon into the environment, adding to ozone depleting substance emanations. Changes in land cover can likewise impact nearby environment designs, affecting temperature, precipitation, and other climatic factors.

3. **Soil Corruption:** Escalated farming practices, deforestation, and different types of land use change can prompt soil debasement. Loss of dirt, supplement consumption, and expanded weakness to disintegration are normal outcomes, influencing the drawn out efficiency of the land.

4. **Water Assets:** Changes in land use can modify water accessibility and quality. Urbanization, horticulture, and deforestation can influence the hydrological cycle, prompting changes in stream, groundwater re-energize, and the gamble of floods or dry seasons.

5. **Social and Social Effects:** Land use change can significantly affect nearby networks and native populaces. Uprooting, loss of customary jobs, and changes in social practices are normal social effects related with enormous scope land use changes.

6. **Financial Results:** While land use change can add to monetary turn of events, it might likewise have negative financial outcomes. Corruption of regular assets, loss of biological system administrations, and the drawn out expenses of natural harm can present financial difficulties.

7. **Flexibility and Variation:** Environments' capacity to adjust to changing circumstances and recuperate from aggravations is impacted by the degree and

nature of land use change. A few biological systems might be stronger to specific sorts of land use change, while others might confront irreversible harm.

8. **Preservation Open doors:** Regardless of the difficulties presented via land use change, there are potential open doors for protection and economical land the board. Key land use arranging, safeguarded region assignment, and the rebuilding of debased lands are instances of intercessions that can alleviate the adverse consequences of land use change.

Moderation and Feasible Land Use Arranging:

Tending to the difficulties presented via land use change requires proactive relief systems and maintainable land use arranging. A few key methodologies include:

1. **Manageable Improvement Objectives:** Adjusting land use arranging with the Unified Countries Practical Advancement Objectives (SDGs) gives a structure to offsetting financial improvement with ecological and social contemplations. Incorporating the SDGs into public and local arrangements can direct manageable land use rehearses.

2. **Safeguarded Regions and Preservation Stores:** Laying out and really overseeing safeguarded regions and protection saves are basic parts of land use arranging. These regions act as shelters for biodiversity, empowering the protection of biological systems and offering fundamental types of assistance like water purging and carbon sequestration.

3. **Biological system Based Variation:** Embracing environment based transformation techniques includes working with normal environments to improve their strength to environmental change and different stressors. This approach perceives the job of sound biological systems in offering fundamental types of assistance and supporting human prosperity.

4. **Agroecology and Feasible Farming:** Advancing agroecological rehearses and supportable agribusiness can assist with diminishing the natural effect of land use change. These practices focus on environmental standards, biodiversity preservation, and the maintainable administration of normal assets.

5. **Reclamation and Reforestation:** Endeavors to reestablish corrupted lands and reforest regions that have encountered deforestation are pivotal for moderating the effects of land use change. Reforestation undertakings can upgrade biodiversity, sequester carbon, and work on neighborhood environments.

6. **Local area Contribution and Native Information:** Including nearby networks, particularly native people groups, in land use dynamic cycles is fundamental. Native information frameworks frequently offer significant bits of knowledge into maintainable land the board rehearses and can add to powerful preservation procedures.

7. **Strategy Mix:** Coordinating area use arrangements with more extensive ecological and social approaches guarantees an all encompassing way to deal with manageable turn of events. Coordination among various areas, like farming, ranger service, and metropolitan preparation, is fundamental for tending to the multi-layered parts of land use change.

Future Patterns and Difficulties:

As the worldwide local area wrestles with the intricacies of land use change, a few future patterns and difficulties arise. These include:

1. **Urbanization and Megacities:** The steady pattern of urbanization is supposed to keep, prompting the extension of megacities and metropolitan regions. Overseeing metropolitan development economically will be a basic test, requiring imaginative ways to deal with offset improvement with natural protection.
2. **Mechanical Developments:** Advances in innovation, including man-made reasoning, remote detecting, and accuracy horticulture, will assume an undeniably huge part in forming land use designs. Outfitting these innovations for supportable practices and checking will be pivotal for successful land use the board.
3. **Environmental Change Transformation:** Environmental change will keep on affecting area use designs, requiring versatile systems to moderate the effects on biological systems and human networks. Anticipating environment strong land use practices will be fundamental for guaranteeing the drawn out maintainability of scenes.
4. **Worldwide Collaboration:** The interconnected idea of land use change requires worldwide participation and composed endeavors. Peaceful accords, for example, those tending to biodiversity protection and environmental change, will be instrumental in cultivating coordinated effort among countries.
5. **Value and Civil rights:** Tending to the social effects of land use change, like dislodging and loss of occupations, requires a pledge to value and civil rights. Comprehensive land use arranging that considers the requirements and points of view of different networks is fundamental for reasonable turn of events.
6. **Strategy Execution and Requirement:** The adequacy of land use approaches relies upon their fruitful execution and authorization. Reinforcing administration systems, guaranteeing straightforwardness, and considering responsible those answerable for land use choices are basic parts of viable arrangement execution.

B. Significance of Conservation Amidst Land Use

In the complex dance between human turn of events and natural safeguarding, the meaning of protection in the midst of advancing area use elements couldn't possibly be more significant. As the worldwide populace thrives, metropolitan regions grow, and farming requests heighten, the fragile harmony between addressing human necessities and defending the normal world turns out to be progressively difficult. This investigation digs into the urgent job of protection amidst dynamic land use designs, featuring its importance for biodiversity, environments, environment versatility, and the prosperity of present and people in the future.

Biodiversity Safeguarding:

Preservation fills in as a foundation in saving the rich embroidery of biodiversity that decorates our planet. Biodiversity is the complex trap of life, including the range of species, biological systems, and hereditary variety. Land use changes, like deforestation, urbanization, and rural development, frequently lead to environment annihilation and discontinuity, bringing about the deficiency of plant and creature species. Preservation endeavors, including the foundation of safeguarded regions, untamed life hallways, and supportable land the board rehearses, are significant for keeping up with biodiversity areas of interest and guaranteeing the endurance of different and frequently jeopardized species.

Environment Administrations and Human Prosperity:

Environments, molded via land use designs, give a heap of administrations fundamental for human prosperity. Clean air, new water, prolific soil, fertilization of yields, and environment guideline are only a couple of instances of biological system benefits that support life on The planet. Protection goes about as a defend for these administrations, guaranteeing that biological systems stay versatile and fit for supporting human social orders. By safeguarding normal living spaces and advancing reasonable land use rehearses, protection contributes straightforwardly to the personal satisfaction, well-being, and success of networks all over the planet.

Environment Flexibility and Moderation:

Land use change, especially deforestation and modifications in vegetation cover, contributes fundamentally to environmental change. Backwoods, for instance, go about as carbon sinks, retaining and putting away a lot of carbon dioxide. At the point when backwoods are cleared for farming or metropolitan turn of events, this put away carbon is delivered into the environment, intensifying the nursery impact. Preservation drives, like afforestation, reforestation, and the security of carbon-rich environments, assume an imperative part in environment flexibility and moderation. By saving and reestablishing normal scenes, protection adds to the worldwide battle against environmental change.

Maintainable Asset The board:

Preservation is characteristically connected to the reasonable administration of regular assets. Land use rehearses that focus on preservation standards guarantee that assets like water, soil, and biodiversity are utilized such that addresses recent concerns without compromising the capacity of people in the future to address their own issues. Feasible agribusiness, agroecological rehearses, and dependable ranger service epitomize approaches that offset human requests with the basic to monitor and recover normal assets.

Social and Tasteful Qualities:

Past its biological importance, preservation holds social and tasteful worth. Numerous native networks have profound associations with explicit scenes, seeing them as sacrosanct and necessary to their character. Protection endeavors that regard and integrate native information add to the safeguarding of social legacy. Also, normal scenes have inherent stylish worth, giving spaces to diversion, motivation, and profound reestablishment. The preservation of grand scenes guarantees that people in the future can keep on determining these social and stylish advantages.

Flexibility to Ecological Changes:

Preservation adds to the versatility of biological systems despite ecological changes, including those incited by environmental change. Various and unblemished biological systems are better prepared to adjust to evolving conditions, endure aggravations, and recuperate from normal occasions like fierce blazes, tempests, and dry seasons. Protection estimates that attention on keeping up with biological system trustworthiness and availability improve the capacity of scenes to return from disturbances, guaranteeing long haul manageability.

Alleviation of Ecological Debasement:

Land use changes, particularly those determined by impractical practices, can prompt ecological debasement. Soil disintegration, loss of biodiversity, water contamination, and the consumption of normal assets are among the outcomes. Protection goes about as a defense against natural corruption by advancing dependable land the executives, territory reclamation, and the reception of feasible practices. Through these endeavors, preservation mitigates the adverse consequences of land use changes and cultivates the recovery of debased biological systems.

C. Purpose and Scope of the Book

The book, named "Exploring the Scene: Understanding the Exchange of Land Use and Preservation," leaves on a complete investigation of the unpredictable connection between human exercises and the climate. Established in the acknowledgment of the significant effect of land use on environments and biodiversity, this work tries to unwind the intricacies, difficulties, and valuable open doors at the crossing point of land use and protection. The reason and extent of the book stretch out past a simple scholarly undertaking, expecting to illuminate, move, and guide perusers towards a more profound comprehension of the elements that shape our planet.

Reason:

The main role of this book is to encourage a comprehensive comprehension of the diverse interaction between land use and preservation. It looks to rise above disciplinary limits, drawing in perusers from different foundations, including natural science, environment, geology, strategy studies, and then some. The overall objective is to engage perusers with the information and experiences expected to explore the intricacies of contemporary land use elements, perceiving the desperation of economical practices despite worldwide natural difficulties.

This work tries to move a feeling of obligation and stewardship, empowering perusers to consider their part in the complicated snare of human-climate communications. By clarifying the outcomes of uncontrolled land use changes and featuring the meaning of protection, the book intends to rouse people, policymakers, and experts to contribute effectively to the aggregate exertion of safeguarding the planet's biodiversity and biological systems.

Scope:

The extent of the book traverses a different exhibit of subjects, enveloping verifiable viewpoints ashore use, contemporary difficulties presented by urbanization and horticultural extension, the job of native information in preservation, the effect of mechanical developments, and the significance of global joint effort. Contextual analyses from various districts enlighten triumphs and disappointments in dealing with the sensitive harmony between human turn of events and ecological safeguarding.

The book digs into the subtleties of land use change, investigating its definitions, drivers, and the ramifications for biodiversity, environment strength, and human prosperity. It consolidates conversations on the job of protection in relieving ecological debasement, cultivating supportable asset the executives, and advancing environment strength. Through an interdisciplinary methodology, the book endeavors to connect holes between logical examination, strategy plan, and local area commitment, perceiving the interconnectedness of these aspects in molding a supportable future.

Generally, "Exploring the Scene" fills in as an aide for perusers exploring the complicated territory of land use and protection. It gives a guide to understanding the difficulties and open doors introduced by human exercises, offering experiences that can illuminate informed direction, motivate preservation drives, and add to an aggregate obligation to defending the planet for present and people in the future.

Chapter 1

Understanding Land Use Change

Understanding area use change is fundamental for fathoming the unique associations between human exercises and the climate. This diverse peculiarity envelops shifts in land cover, modifications in land the board rehearses, and the change of regular territories into anthropogenic scenes. A nuanced investigation of land use change includes looking at its verifiable roots, drivers, effects, and expected pathways towards supportability. This far reaching understanding is vital as we explore a time set apart by populace development, innovative headways, and worldwide requests for assets.

Authentic Points of view Ashore Use Change:

To get a handle on the ongoing elements of land use transform, it is basic to dig into its verifiable setting. Conventional social orders frequently rehearsed feasible land use, keeping a sensitive harmony between asset usage and protection. In any case, the industrialization and modernization of the nineteenth and twentieth hundreds of years achieved quick and groundbreaking changes. The getting free from timberlands for agribusiness, metropolitan extension, and asset extraction became characterizing elements of human exercises, making way for the escalation of land use changes in ongoing many years.

Definition and Aspects of Land Use Change:

Land use change includes noticeable adjustments in the reason or the executives of land after some time. It exemplifies a range of exercises, including the transformation of regular scenes to metropolitan regions, changes in rural practices, and changes in land residency frameworks. The two essential classifications of land use change are transformation, including a progress starting with one land use type then onto the next, and increase, zeroing in on more proficient or heightened utilization of existing area.

Drivers of Land Use Change:

Land use change is driven by a mind boggling interaction of social, financial, political, and natural elements. Populace development, agrarian extension, urbanization, framework improvement, mechanical headways, monetary contemplations, strategy and administration, and environmental change all add to the mind boggling embroidered artwork of land use elements. Understanding these drivers is essential for forming viable techniques that offset human requirements with natural manageability.

Effects of Land Use Change:

The effects of land use change are significant and interconnected, influencing biological systems, biodiversity, environment, water assets, and human social orders. Biodiversity misfortune, environmental change commitment, soil corruption, adjustments in water assets, social and social effects, financial results, expanded hazard of cataclysmic events, and the deficiency of biological system administrations are among the diverse outcomes of land use change. These effects highlight the requirement for all encompassing ways to deal with address the intricacies emerging from human-climate connections.

Alleviation and Transformation Methodologies:

Moderating the effects of land use change requires a blend of methodologies pointed toward lessening or forestalling unfortunate results. Reasonable land the executives rehearses, the foundation and viable administration of safeguarded regions, afforestation, reforestation, and mindful ranger service rehearses are necessary parts of relief endeavors. Also, variation methodologies center around improving the strength of environments and networks to adapt to evolving conditions. These incorporate the reclamation of corrupted lands, the advancement of agroecological approaches, and the combination of native information into land use arranging.

Remote Detecting and Checking Area Use Change:

The coming of remote detecting innovation has reformed our capacity to screen and measure land use change for an enormous scope. Satellite symbolism, geographic data frameworks (GIS), and other remote detecting apparatuses empower scientists to follow changes in land cover with accuracy. These advances give important information to surveying the degree and effect of land use change, working with informed direction and strategy improvement. Constant checking offers experiences into spatial examples and patterns, adding to an extensive comprehension of the elements of land use change.

Contextual investigations: Gaining from Progress and Disappointment:

Looking at contextual analyses from different locales offers important experiences into the mind boggling interaction between land use and protection. Examples of overcoming adversity, like the recuperation of jeopardized species or the rebuilding of corrupted scenes, give motivation and illustrations to future protection endeavors. On the other hand, occurrences of disappointment and unseen side-effects highlight the requirement for versatile administration and a nuanced comprehension of nearby settings. Contextual analyses might incorporate instances of maintainable land use rehearses, local area drove protection drives, or occasions where financial turn of events and preservation objectives have been effectively coordinated.

Breaking down both positive and adverse results adds to a more thorough comprehension of the difficulties and open doors intrinsic in the connection between land use and preservation.

Future Possibilities and Arising Difficulties:

In the Anthropocene time, portrayed by phenomenal human impact in the world, the fate of land use and preservation is at a junction. Arising difficulties, for example, the rising interest for assets, environmental change influences, and the potential for novel advancements to reshape scenes, require ground breaking techniques. The joining of preservation standards into arising fields, like manageable metropolitan plan, round economies, and regenerative farming, holds guarantee for a more reasonable future. Saddling the force of development, encouraging interdisciplinary cooperation, and drawing in neighborhood networks in preservation endeavors are key parts of a strong and versatile way to deal with land use. What's in store requests a comprehensive comprehension of the perplexing collaborations between human social orders and the climate, with a pledge to encouraging an amicable conjunction that supports biodiversity and guarantees the prosperity of people in the future.

1.1 Types and Drivers of Land Use Change

Land use change is a dynamic and diverse peculiarity driven by a complicated interaction of variables that shape the World's scenes. Understanding the sorts and drivers of land use change is significant for disentangling the intricacies of human-climate collaborations. This investigation digs into the different elements of land use change, ordering types and analyzing the drivers move these changes. From urbanization and rural extension to foundation advancement and mechanical developments, the powers guiding area use change are different and interconnected.

Kinds of Land Use Change:

Urbanization:

Urbanization addresses a critical sort of land use change portrayed by the development of metropolitan regions. As populaces incline toward urban communities looking for financial open doors, never-ending suburbia infringes upon normal scenes. This cycle includes the transformation of farming area, woods, or other regular natural surroundings into developed regions, bringing about modified land cover, expanded impenetrable surfaces, and changes in the metropolitan rustic connection point.

Agrarian Extension:

Horticultural extension is a predominant driver of land use change, including the transformation of regular biological systems into developed lands.

Backwoods, prairies, and different living spaces are frequently cleared to clear a path for huge scope horticulture, driven by the developing interest for food and products. This sort of land use change can prompt biodiversity misfortune, soil corruption, and changes in hydrological designs.

Foundation Advancement:

The development of framework, like streets, roadways, dams, and metropolitan conveniences, requires changes in land use. Foundation improvement frequently includes the change of land for transportation, energy, and water the board projects. While these advancements add to monetary development, they can prompt territory discontinuity, adjusted waste examples, and ecological debasement.

Deforestation:

Deforestation includes the getting free from timberlands for different purposes, including agribusiness, logging, and framework improvement. This sort of land use change has significant ramifications for biodiversity, carbon sequestration, and environment guideline. The deficiency of woodlands adds to ozone depleting substance discharges and upsets complex environmental connections inside these biological systems.

Mining and Extraction:

Mining exercises bring about significant land use changes, changing regular scenes into extraction locales. The evacuation of minerals, oil, or gas modifies the geology and can prompt soil disintegration, environment annihilation, and tainting of encompassing biological systems. The natural effects of mining add to durable changes in land use designs.

Wetland Transformation:

Wetland transformation includes the depleting or filling of wetlands for horticulture, metropolitan turn of events, or framework projects. This change upsets the special natural elements of wetlands, affecting water filtration, flood control, and territory arrangement. The deficiency of wetlands has flowing consequences for biodiversity and can intensify the gamble of flooding.

Country to Metropolitan Change:

The progress from rustic to metropolitan scenes addresses a particular kind of land use change set apart by the change of rural or regular regions into metropolitan conditions. This cycle includes changes in land cover, the production of metropolitan framework, and modifications in the financial texture of the impacted areas.

Land Surrender and Reforestation:

Rather than land use change driven by development, deserting of agrarian terrains can bring about reforestation or normal recovery. This sort of land use change might happen because of monetary movements, changes in farming practices, or provincial to-metropolitan relocation. It can add to natural rebuilding, carbon sequestration, and biodiversity recuperation.

Drivers of Land Use Change:

Populace Development:

The total populace keeps on extending, putting expanded expectations ashore for lodging, food creation, and framework. Populace development is a basic driver of land use change, pushing social orders to change over regular scenes into metropolitan regions, horticultural fields, and other human-ruled spaces.

Horticultural Interest:

The need to take care of a developing populace drives changes in land use, with horticultural extension being a critical result. Expanding interest for food and products prompts the transformation of normal territories into croplands, influencing biological systems, biodiversity, and soil wellbeing.

Urbanization:

Urbanization is a strong driver of land use change as individuals relocate to urban communities looking for business and worked on expectations for everyday comforts. The development of metropolitan regions prompts the transformation of country scenes into assembled conditions, causing changes in land cover, expanded impenetrable surfaces, and modified biological system elements.

Foundation Advancement:

The development of foundation, including streets, extensions, and dams, impacts land use designs. Foundation advancement is much of the time driven by financial development and the requirement for availability, adding to the change of land for transportation, energy, and water the board projects.

Monetary Elements:

Monetary contemplations, for example, market interest for explicit wares, assume an essential part in molding land use choices. Benefit intentions can drive the transformation of normal scenes into regions more appropriate for monetary exercises, including horticulture, mining, and metropolitan turn of events.

Mechanical Advancements:

Propels in innovation, remembering enhancements for farming, transportation, and asset extraction, impact land use designs. Mechanical developments can prompt changes in land the executives works on, adjusting the force and proficiency of asset use.

Strategy and Administration:

Government arrangements and guidelines altogether influence land use change. Land residency frameworks, protection strategies, and drafting guidelines impact how land is used and made due. The adequacy of these strategies can either work with reasonable land use or add to ecological corruption.

Environmental Change:

Changes in environment examples can impact land use by adjusting the reasonableness of regions for specific exercises. Changes in temperature, precipitation, and outrageous climate occasions might affect farming reasonableness, water assets, and environment elements, impacting land use choices.

Social and Social Elements:

Social qualities, social elements, and segment patterns impact land use change. Conventional land use rehearses, social impression of scenes, and social designs can shape choices connected with farming, urbanization, and protection.

Globalization:

Globalization, set apart by expanded interconnectedness and the development of products and individuals across borders, impacts land use change. Worldwide business sectors drive interest for explicit items, prompting changes in land use to meet global exchange necessities.

Land Possession and Residency Frameworks:

The construction of land proprietorship and residency frameworks assumes a basic part in deciding how land is used. Land use choices are impacted by elements, for example, land residency security, property freedoms, and common land the board rehearses.

Struggle and Political Precariousness:

Struggle and political precariousness can bring about quick and impromptu changes in land use. Relocation of populaces, asset abuse during clashes, and changes in administration structures add to adjustments in land cover and land the board.

Customer Conduct and Inclinations:

Customer inclinations and conduct, including decisions connected with diet, lodging, and way of life, impact land use designs. For instance, changes in purchaser interest for explicit rural items can drive changes in land use for development.

Mechanical Advancements:

Progresses in innovation, including computerized reasoning, accuracy farming, and remote detecting, are progressively affecting area use choices. These developments give new apparatuses to observing, making due, and enhancing land use, adding to both positive and adverse consequences on the climate.

1.2 Global and Regional Patterns

Land use change is a worldwide peculiarity that appears in different local examples, mirroring the unique exchange between human exercises and natural variables. Understanding the worldwide and local elements of land use change is significant for contriving powerful systems that offset human advancement with preservation objectives. This investigation digs into the all-encompassing worldwide examples of land use change and looks at how these patterns manifest in various areas, taking into account factors, for example, financial elements, natural circumstances, and social impacts.

Worldwide Examples of Land Use Change:

Urbanization Patterns:

All around the world, one of the most prominent examples of land use change is the tireless pattern of urbanization. Quick populace development, combined with country to-metropolitan relocation, has prompted the extension of metropolitan regions. Megacities and metropolitan locales are central marks of this change, with broad land transformation from regular scenes to constructed conditions. The spatial impression of urbanization adjusts land cover, upsets biological systems, and stances challenges for maintainable metropolitan preparation.

Rural Heightening:

Horticulture stays a predominant power driving area use change worldwide. The interest for food, combined with innovative progressions, has prompted the strengthening of farming practices. Enormous scope monoculture, automation, and the utilization of agrochemicals add to the change of regular living spaces into profoundly oversaw farming terrains. This example has suggestions for biodiversity, soil wellbeing, and water assets.

Deforestation Areas of interest:

Deforestation, especially in tropical locales, addresses a basic worldwide land use change design. Timberlands, frequently alluded to as the lungs of the Earth, face significant dangers from logging, farming extension, and foundation improvement. Deforestation areas of interest incorporate the Amazon rainforest, Southeast Asian timberlands, and the Congo Bowl. The deficiency of these biodiverse environments adds to environmental change, biodiversity decline, and disturbance of neighborhood and worldwide biological systems.

Foundation Advancement Hallways:

Worldwide availability requests broad framework advancement, prompting the making of halls that navigate assorted scenes. Thruways, rail routes, and other vehicle networks cut across areas, bringing about land use changes to oblige these passageways. Framework improvement passageways can work with monetary development yet frequently come to the detriment of normal living spaces, raising worries about environment fracture and biodiversity misfortune.

Preservation and Safeguarded Regions:

Simultaneous with land use changes that undermine biological systems, there is a worldwide work to lay out preservation and safeguarded regions. These regions act as shelters for biodiversity, giving basic territories to imperiled species. The foundation of marine safeguarded regions, public parks, and untamed life saves mirrors a counterexample to anthropogenic land use changes, stressing the requirement for protection despite worldwide difficulties.

Local Examples of Land Use Change:

North America:

In North America, land use change is portrayed by a verifiable tradition of urbanization, horticultural extension, and foundation improvement. Tremendous spreads of rural land in the US and Canada add to a critical impression of land devoted to food creation. Endless suburbia, particularly in locales with high populace thickness, brings about the transformation of regular scenes to rural and metropolitan regions. Preservation endeavors in North America center around safeguarding naturally significant areas, like public parks and untamed life passageways.

Europe:

Europe encounters a complicated example of land use change impacted by verifiable, social, and monetary variables. Rural practices, frequently molded by hundreds of years of land use, have prompted a mosaic of scenes going from customary farmland to reforested regions.

Urbanization is articulated in thickly populated districts, with noteworthy urban communities frequently venturing into encompassing country scenes. As of late, there has been an accentuation on economical land the executives rehearses and the reclamation of debased lands.

Asia:

Asia shows assorted territorial examples of land use change because of varieties in populace thickness, financial turn of events, and social practices. Fast urbanization is especially unmistakable in nations like China and India, where blossoming populaces drive the development of megacities. Horticultural development, remembering huge scope development and moving development for certain areas, adds to changes in land cover. Southeast Asia faces difficulties from deforestation driven by logging and palm oil ranches, affecting the rich biodiversity of the area.

Africa:

Africa encounters a mix of customary land use practices and contemporary difficulties. Rural development, frequently determined by means cultivating, coincides with huge scope foundation activities and urbanization in select locales. Deforestation, driven by logging and agribusiness, presents dangers to the landmass' interesting biological systems. Preservation endeavors in Africa frequently center around safeguarding untamed life and protecting basic territories, especially in regions with high biodiversity.

South America:

South America, home to the Amazon rainforest, faces serious strain from agrarian extension, logging, and framework improvement. The Amazon, frequently alluded to as the "lungs of the Earth," is a point of convergence of worldwide worry because of far reaching deforestation. Horticultural exercises, including dairy cattle farming and soy development, add to enormous scope land use changes. Preservation drives in South America mean to alleviate deforestation, safeguard native regions, and lay out feasible land the executives rehearses.

Factors Impacting Local Examples:

Financial Elements:

Financial elements, including populace thickness, pay levels, and work open doors, altogether impact provincial examples of land use change. Urbanization will in general be more articulated in areas with high populace thickness and quick monetary development, while horticultural extension might be driven by the requirement for food security and financial turn of events.

Social Practices:

Social practices and customary land use techniques assume a vital part in forming provincial examples. Native people group frequently take part in feasible land the board rehearses that have developed over ages. Social qualities connected with nature preservation might impact the foundation of safeguarded regions and the conservation of conventional scenes.

Strategy and Administration:

The strategies and administration designs of individual nations and locales direct the direction of land use change. Severe preservation approaches, feasible land the executives rehearses, and viable land-use arranging can alleviate adverse consequences. Conversely, frail administration might prompt unregulated double-dealing of regular assets and impractical land use rehearses.

Environment and Natural Circumstances:

Provincial environment and natural circumstances impact land use designs. Bone-dry locales might encounter difficulties connected with water shortage and desertification, affecting agrarian practices. Waterfront regions are helpless to changes in land use because of urbanization and framework advancement driven by the vicinity to oceanic shipping lanes.

Globalization:

The globalization of business sectors and exchange impacts provincial land use designs. Interest for explicit products on the worldwide market can drive rural development, logging, and mining exercises in specific districts. Worldwide monetary interconnectedness adds to the transmission of land use changes across borders.

Innovative Progressions:

Mechanical headways, remembering enhancements for agribusiness, transportation, and remote detecting, influence local land use designs. Accuracy horticulture practices might upgrade the effectiveness of land use in specific districts, while headways in transportation foundation might work with admittance to beforehand far off regions.

1.3 Historical Context and Trends

Understanding the authentic setting of land use change is fundamental for grasping the ongoing direction of human-climate communications. Since the beginning of time, the connection among social orders and their scenes has gone through critical changes, formed by social, mechanical, and monetary elements. This investigation digs into the verifiable setting of land use change, following the advancement of human practices and their effect on scenes.

Analyzing authentic patterns gives important experiences into the underlying foundations of contemporary difficulties and illuminates techniques for reasonable land use from now on.

Antiquated Agrarian Practices:

The starting points of land use change can be followed back to the beginning of horticulture, denoting a vital defining moment in mankind's set of experiences. The change from migrant agrarian ways of life to settled horticultural networks on a very basic level modified the connection among people and the land. Antiquated civilizations, like those in Mesopotamia, the Indus Valley, and the Nile Delta, created modern water system frameworks and terraced agribusiness, reshaping scenes to help developing populaces.

Middle age Rural Extension:

During the middle age time frame, farming extension turned into a predominant power in molding land use. The development of primitive social orders in Europe prompted the freedom of woodlands for horticulture, mirroring a shift from resource cultivating to more escalated land use rehearses. The development of immense regions for harvests and animals essentially changed the European scene, adding to the arrangement of agrarian social orders.

Expansionism and the Time of Investigation:

The time of investigation and expansionism further escalated land use change. European powers, looking for new shipping lanes and assets, extended their domains across the Americas, Africa, and Asia. This period saw enormous scope deforestation, the presentation of money crops, and the uprooting of native land the executives rehearses. The effect of expansionism ashore use is significant, with enduring ramifications for biodiversity, environments, and native networks.

Modern Transformation and Urbanization:

The Modern Upheaval, traversing the late eighteenth to mid nineteenth hundreds of years, denoted a groundbreaking period in mankind's set of experiences. The automation of agribusiness, the ascent of processing plants, and the development of metropolitan focuses prompted uncommon changes in land use. Urbanization turned into a characterizing pattern as individuals relocated from provincial regions to urban communities looking for business. The transformation of farming area to modern and metropolitan purposes changed scenes on a worldwide scale.

20th Century Farming Heightening:

The 20th century saw a change in outlook in horticultural practices with the coming of mechanical developments. The Green Transformation, beginning during the twentieth hundred years, presented high-yielding harvest assortments, engineered composts, and pesticides, decisively expanding agrarian efficiency. While this upheaval added to food security, it additionally prompted the increase of land use, with the extension of monoculture and the utilization of substance inputs.

Post-The Second Great War Urbanization and Suburbanization:

The post-The Second Great War time saw extraordinary urbanization and suburbanization patterns. The time of increased birth rates, combined with financial thriving in numerous Western nations, powered the interest for lodging and framework. Rural spread, portrayed by the development of neighborhoods into beforehand lacking scenes, turned into a noticeable element of land use change. This pattern changed normal scenes as well as added to issues of natural debasement and asset utilization.

Late twentieth Century Protection Mindfulness:

The last 50% of the 20th century likewise saw a developing consciousness of ecological preservation. Worries about biodiversity misfortune, deforestation, and contamination incited the foundation of ecological developments and protection associations. Endeavors to assign safeguarded regions, direct asset extraction, and advance reasonable land the executives rehearses picked up speed, mirroring a shift toward perceiving the significance of preservation despite raising area use changes.

Twenty-First Century Elements:

In the twenty-first hundred years, land use change elements have become progressively complicated and interconnected. Globalization, innovative progressions, and the continuous test of offsetting financial improvement with ecological supportability shape contemporary patterns. Urbanization keeps on speeding up, especially in creating locales, adding to the development of megacities and the transformation of farming area to metropolitan purposes. Horticultural practices are developing with the coordination of accuracy cultivating, agroecology, and economical land the board standards.

Key Patterns in Contemporary Land Use Change:

Proceeded with Urbanization:

Urbanization stays a predominant pattern in land use change, with an expected 68% of the worldwide populace projected to live in metropolitan regions by 2050. Fast urbanization presents difficulties connected with foundation advancement, asset utilization, and the deficiency of normal environments.

Savvy metropolitan preparation and supportable improvement rehearses are significant for alleviating the adverse consequences of urbanization.

Escalation of Agribusiness:

Farming strengthening keeps on molding land use designs, driven by the need to take care of a developing worldwide populace. Accuracy horticulture, hereditary designing, and the reception of feasible cultivating rehearses are arising patterns. Adjusting the requirement for expanded food creation with ecological protection is a basic test in contemporary land use elements.

Mechanical Developments:

Mechanical progressions, including remote detecting, man-made reasoning, and blockchain, are impacting land use change observing and the executives. Remote detecting apparatuses give significant information to surveying changes in land cover, observing deforestation, and executing accuracy horticulture rehearses. These advancements offer open doors for informed dynamic in land use arranging.

Sustainable power Change:

The change to environmentally friendly power sources is impacting land use designs. Huge scope sun powered and wind energy projects require critical land regions, bringing up issues about their effect on biological systems and biodiversity. Finding some kind of harmony between environmentally friendly power advancement and protection is essential for accomplishing manageable energy objectives.

Preservation and Maintainable Practices:

Preservation endeavors and maintainable land the executives rehearses are acquiring unmistakable quality. The foundation of safeguarded regions, reforestation drives, and the advancement of agroecological approaches mirror a developing acknowledgment of the need to offset human exercises with biological protection. Local area drove preservation drives and cooperative endeavors between states, NGOs, and nearby networks are forming contemporary protection patterns.

Environmental Change Transformation:

The effects of environmental change, including increasing temperatures, changing precipitation examples, and outrageous climate occasions, impact land use choices. Transformation methodologies, like moving rural works on, carrying out environment versatile framework, and planning metropolitan spaces for expanded environment strength, are becoming necessary parts of land use arranging.

Difficulties and Potential open doors:

Biodiversity Misfortune and Living space Fracture:

Biodiversity misfortune and environment discontinuity stay basic difficulties related with land use change. The transformation of regular natural surroundings into metropolitan, horticultural, or modern scenes disturbs biological systems, prompting the downfall of plant and creature species. Protection methodologies and living space reclamation endeavors are fundamental for relieving these effects.

Food Security and Economical Farming:

Satisfying the developing worldwide need for food while guaranteeing supportable horticulture rehearses represents a huge test. Finding some kind of harmony between expanding agrarian efficiency and limiting ecological effects requires the reception of agroecological approaches, accuracy cultivating, and the combination of feasible land the board rehearses.

Fair Metropolitan Turn of events:

Urbanization patterns should resolve issues of fair turn of events, guaranteeing that the advantages of metropolitan development are divided between assorted populaces. Comprehensive metropolitan preparation, reasonable lodging, and green foundation drives add to establishing manageable and bearable metropolitan conditions.

Environmental Change Moderation and Variation:

Land use assumes an essential part in environmental change moderation and transformation. Safeguarding woods, carrying out reforestation projects, and taking on economical land the board rehearses add to carbon sequestration and environment strength. Coordinated approaches that consider both environmental change and land use elements are fundamental for tending to these interconnected difficulties.

Local area Commitment and Native Information:

Comprehensive land use arranging includes dynamic commitment with neighborhood networks and the joining of native information. Perceiving the stewardship of native networks over their properties and incorporating customary practices into protection and land the executives endeavors add to additional manageable results.

Strategy and Administration:

Viable strategies and administration structures are crucial for molding economical land use rehearses. Land use arranging that thinks about natural, social, and financial aspects, alongside powerful guidelines and requirement components, is fundamental for directing improvement in a way that offsets human necessities with environmental supportability.

Chapter 2

The Impact Of Land Use Change On Biodiversity

Land use change, driven by human exercises and financial elements, is a powerful power molding the World's scenes. While it frequently serves human requirements for lodging, agribusiness, and framework, its repercussions on biodiversity are significant and extensive. Biodiversity, enveloping the assortment of life on The planet, assumes a urgent part in biological system wellbeing, flexibility, and the arrangement of environment administrations. This investigation digs into the complicated transaction between land use change and biodiversity, looking at the systems, results, and potential relief techniques notwithstanding this complex environmental test.

Characterizing Biodiversity:

Biodiversity is a complex idea embodying the assortment of life at different hierarchical levels - from qualities and species to environments. It envelops hereditary variety inside populaces, species variety inside biological systems, and the variety of environments themselves. Biodiversity isn't just a proportion of the lavishness of life yet in addition an impression of the complicated communications and interdependencies that support environments and add to the general wellbeing of the planet.

Systems of Effect:

Natural surroundings Misfortune and Fracture:

One of the essential systems through which land use change influences biodiversity is territory misfortune and fracture. The change of normal territories into metropolitan regions, horticultural fields, or modern zones straightforwardly decreases the accessible living space for incalculable species. Fracture further compounds this effect by disengaging populaces, upsetting relocation courses, and impeding the progression of qualities between divided patches.

Deforestation and Environment Change:

Deforestation, driven by logging, rural extension, and foundation improvement, is a significant driver of biodiversity misfortune. Woodlands, portrayed by high species variety, give environment to various plant and creature species. Clear-cutting and transformation of timberlands into monoculture ranches or metropolitan regions bring about the deficiency of individual species as well as whole environmental networks.

Contamination and Territory Corruption:

Land use change frequently brings contaminations into biological systems, prompting environment debasement and adversely influencing biodiversity. Farming spillover containing pesticides and composts, modern effluents, and metropolitan poisons can defile water bodies, soil, and air, influencing the strength of species and adjusting environment elements.

Environmental Change Cooperations:

Land use change is complicatedly connected with environmental change, and the two peculiarities apply synergistic effects on biodiversity. Changes in land cover, like deforestation, add to modifications in nearby and local environments. In the mean time, environmental change impacts the appropriateness of natural surroundings for species, driving them to move or adjust to new circumstances, further compounding the difficulties presented via land use change.

Obtrusive Species Presentation:

Land use change can work with the presentation and spread of obtrusive species. As normal living spaces are adjusted, obtrusive species might track down new specialties and outcompete local vegetation. The presence of obtrusive species can prompt disturbances in environmental cycles, predation pressures, and the dislodging of local species, adding to biodiversity decline.

Overharvesting and Asset Abuse:

Certain land use changes, especially those connected with asset abuse, can prompt overharvesting of untamed life and exhaustion of normal assets. Unreasonable logging, overfishing, and hunting practices can drive species to the edge of eradication, disturbing biological equilibriums and lessening biodiversity.

Results of Biodiversity Misfortune:

Environment Dependability and Versatility:

Biodiversity is basic to the dependability and versatility of environments. Various biological systems are better prepared to endure natural vacillations, recuperate from unsettling influences, and adjust to evolving conditions. The deficiency of biodiversity debilitates these limits, delivering biological systems more helpless against illnesses, obtrusive species, and different stressors.

Monetary Effects:

Biodiversity misfortune has direct monetary ramifications, especially for networks reliant upon regular assets. Fisheries, farming, and ranger service, among different areas, depend on assorted environments for their efficiency.

The decay of key species, like pollinators or industrially important fish, can prompt diminished yields, monetary misfortunes, and expanded weakness for networks depending on these assets.

Human Wellbeing Dangers:

Biodiversity misfortune can have backhanded ramifications for human wellbeing. Environment administrations given by different biological systems, like clean water, fertilization of harvests, and regular illness guideline, add to human prosperity. The disturbance of these administrations because of biodiversity misfortune might expand the gamble of waterborne sicknesses, food deficiencies, and other wellbeing related difficulties.

Social and Stylish Worth:

Biodiversity holds huge social and tasteful incentive for social orders around the world. Many societies have profound associations with explicit species or environments, and biodiversity adds to the tasteful satisfaction and sporting encounters of people. The deficiency of novel species and biological systems lessens social variety and denies social orders of the natural benefit of living in a biodiverse world.

Loss of Biodiversity Areas of interest:

Biodiversity areas of interest, locales with especially high species variety and endemism, are especially helpless against land use change. The deficiency of these areas of interest connotes the elimination of novel species as well as subverts worldwide biodiversity. Areas of interest, for example, the Amazon rainforest and coral reefs, assume a lopsided part in keeping up with worldwide environmental equilibrium.

Relief and Protection Systems:

Safeguarded Regions and Protection Stores:

Laying out and really overseeing safeguarded regions and protection saves is a foundation of biodiversity preservation. These assigned spaces give asylum to species, permitting them to flourish without direct dangers from land use change. Very much oversaw safeguarded regions add to the protection of biodiversity areas of interest and the reclamation of biological systems.

Economical Land Use Practices:

Embracing maintainable land use rehearses is fundamental for relieving the effect of human exercises on biodiversity. Feasible farming, agroforestry, and capable logging practices can keep up with biological honesty while addressing human requirements. Incorporating protection standards into metropolitan arranging likewise adds to making practical and biodiversity-accommodating scenes.

Reclamation and Reforestation:

Reclamation endeavors, including reforestation and territory recovery, are urgent for turning around the effects of land use change. Replanting local vegetation, reestablishing debased biological systems, and reconnecting divided living spaces add to the recuperation of biodiversity. Reclamation drives frequently include local area commitment and the reconciliation of nearby information.

Local area Based Protection:

Drawing in nearby networks in preservation endeavors is central for making long haul progress. Local area based preservation includes engaging nearby partners, regarding conventional information, and integrating native practices into land the board methodologies. This approach encourages a feeling of pride and stewardship, adjusting preservation objectives to the necessities and desires of networks.

Biodiversity-Accommodating Arrangements:

Executing and implementing arrangements that focus on biodiversity preservation is urgent. These arrangements might incorporate guidelines against natural surroundings annihilation, limits on asset extraction, and motivators for reasonable land use rehearses. States, in a joint effort with worldwide associations, assume a focal part in creating and upholding such strategies.

Environmental Change Moderation:

Addressing environmental change is indispensable to biodiversity protection, given the mind boggling linkages between the two. Alleviating environmental change includes decreasing ozone depleting substance emanations and carrying out procedures to adjust to changing climatic circumstances. By tending to environmental change, we add to saving the living spaces and conditions that help biodiversity.

Schooling and Mindfulness:

Schooling and mindfulness building drives are fundamental parts of biodiversity preservation. Cultivating a comprehension of the interconnectedness between land use change and biodiversity misfortune engages people and networks to settle on informed decisions. Public help for protection measures is much of the time reinforced through mindfulness crusades and natural instruction.

Contextual analyses:

Amazon Rainforest:

The Amazon rainforest, frequently alluded to as the "lungs of the Earth," faces broad land use change, essentially determined by deforestation for farming and logging.

The deficiency of biodiversity around here, home to various endemic species, has worldwide ramifications for environment guideline and biological system administrations. Preservation endeavors include laying out safeguarded regions, supporting native land privileges, and advancing economical land use rehearses.

Extraordinary Obstruction Reef:

The Incomparable Obstruction Reef, the world's biggest coral reef framework, is profoundly helpless to land-based contamination and environmental change. Spillover from agribusiness presents poisons that hurt coral wellbeing, while at the same time increasing ocean temperatures add to coral dying. Preservation drives center around decreasing contamination, carrying out reasonable agribusiness rehearses, and addressing environmental change to protect the rich biodiversity of the reef.

to offset agrarian efficiency with the preservation of biodiversity.

African Savannahs:

African savannahs, known for their notorious natural life, are encountering land use changes because of farming, domesticated animals touching, and foundation improvement. This effects transitory examples of enormous herbivores and disturbs the sensitive harmony among hunters and prey. Local area based preservation drives, supportable the travel industry, and land-use arranging are utilized to alleviate the effect on biodiversity in these districts.

European Farmlands:

The heightening of agribusiness in European farmlands has prompted environment misfortune for some species, especially those ward on conventional cultivating rehearses. Agri-ecological plans, which boost ranchers to take on biodiversity-accommodating practices, have been executed to alleviate the effect. These plans point

2.1 Habitat Loss and Fragmentation

Territory misfortune and fracture are among the most squeezing difficulties confronting environments around the world, significantly influencing biodiversity and biological system working. Driven basically by human exercises like urbanization, farming, and foundation advancement, these cycles adjust the spatial plan and accessibility of territories, upsetting the sensitive equilibrium that supports assorted types of life. This investigation digs into the complexities of territory misfortune and discontinuity, unwinding the environmental ramifications, investigating basic instruments, and talking about potential moderation methodologies to resolve these basic issues.

Characterizing Environment Misfortune and Fracture:

Environment Misfortune:

Environment misfortune alludes to the decrease in the degree or nature of a characteristic territory, frequently because of the transformation of land for human purposes. This can result from exercises like metropolitan extension, horticulture, logging, or modern turn of events. As regular scenes are changed into metropolitan regions, croplands, or other human-overwhelmed conditions, the first environment is lost, prompting a decrease in the accessibility of reasonable living spaces for plant and creature species.

Living space Fracture:

Living space fracture happens when a constant, solid territory is separated into more modest, disengaged fixes or sections. This discontinuity cycle is in many cases a result of territory misfortune, yet it can likewise happen freely because of foundation improvement, street development, or other straight elements that make obstructions inside the scene. These sections might be encircled by adjusted or ungracious conditions, prompting disconnected populaces and upsetting natural network.

Instruments of Environment Misfortune and Fracture:

Urbanization:

Urbanization is an essential driver of living space misfortune, as normal scenes are changed over into metropolitan regions to oblige the developing human populace. The development of urban areas and foundation brings about the immediate loss of territories, frequently uprooting local widely varied vegetation. Also, metropolitan regions make obstructions to natural life development, adding to living space fracture.

Rural Extension:

Agrarian practices, while fundamental for food creation, contribute altogether to environment misfortune and fracture. The change of woods, fields, and wetlands into croplands or field lessens the accessibility of regular environments. Enormous scope monoculture and automated cultivating further strengthen these effects, prompting the fracture of once-adjacent biological systems.

Foundation Improvement:

The development of streets, expressways, and other framework undertakings can piece natural surroundings and block untamed life development. Straight highlights, for example, transportation passageways, go about as boundaries that seclude populaces and upset natural cycles. Fracture brought about by foundation advancement can prompt expanded mortality, diminished hereditary variety, and modified species circulations.

Logging and Deforestation:

Logging and deforestation add to territory misfortune, especially in forested environments. Clear-cutting for lumber, paper creation, or to make space for agribusiness brings about the immediate evacuation of territories. The leftover patches of woods might be divided, influencing species that require huge, adjoining regions for their endurance.

Mining and Asset Extraction:

Asset extraction exercises, including mining and oil extraction, lead to broad territory corruption and misfortune. The disturbance brought about by these exercises straightforwardly eliminates territories as well as result in contamination, modified hydrology, and other ecological changes that further add to natural surroundings discontinuity.

Environmental Change:

While not an immediate reason for natural surroundings misfortune and discontinuity, environmental change can intensify these cycles. Changes in temperature, precipitation examples, and ocean levels can compel species to move their reaches, looking for reasonable environments. Now and again, this can prompt segregated populaces and divided environments as species move to follow their favored environment conditions.

Biological Ramifications of Natural surroundings Misfortune and Fracture:
Loss of Biodiversity:

Maybe the main biological outcome of natural surroundings misfortune and discontinuity is the deficiency of biodiversity. As territories are diminished in size and accessibility, populaces of plants and creatures decline, and a few animal types might confront elimination. Divided scenes frequently support less species and are more helpless to the effects of obtrusive species.

Hereditary Variety Decrease:

Territory discontinuity can prompt confined populaces that experience diminished quality stream. This segregation might bring about expanded hereditary float and inbreeding, prompting diminished hereditary variety inside populaces. Low hereditary variety makes species more helpless against sicknesses, natural changes, and diminishes their versatile limit.

Adjusted Environment Capabilities:

Flawless environments give a scope of biological system administrations, including water decontamination, fertilization, and environment guideline. Territory misfortune and discontinuity can change these environment capabilities.

For instance, the deficiency of timberland cover can disturb water cycles and lead to changes in nearby environments, affecting both natural life and human networks.

Disturbance of Environmental Cycles:

Living space fracture can upset basic biological cycles like fertilization, seed dispersal, and hunter prey collaborations. Species that rely upon these cycles might be adversely impacted, prompting flowing effects all through the environment. For example, the decay of pollinators can influence the multiplication of blossoming plants, affecting different species in the environment.

Expanded Edge Impacts:

The edges of natural surroundings pieces, known as ecotones, frequently experience special ecological circumstances, known as edge impacts. These circumstances, including adjusted temperature, stickiness, and light levels, can lean toward specific species while disadvantaging others. Expanded predation and rivalry at natural surroundings edges can additionally affect the elements of the environment.

Diminished Environment Flexibility:

Divided natural surroundings are for the most part less versatile to ecological unsettling influences like fierce blazes, tempests, or illness episodes. More modest, secluded populaces are more defenseless to neighborhood terminations, and divided scenes might battle to recuperate from aggravations. This diminished flexibility makes biological systems more defenseless against long haul corruption.

Alleviation Systems and Preservation Approaches:

Passageway Creation:

Laying out untamed life halls that interface divided environments can upgrade biological availability. These passageways give pathways to species to move between detached patches, working with quality stream, and supporting the general soundness of populaces. Very much planned halls can moderate the adverse consequences of territory discontinuity.

Safeguarded Regions and Protection Stores:

Assigning and really overseeing safeguarded regions and protection holds are critical for shielding territories from additional corruption. These regions give asylums to species to flourish without direct dangers from human exercises. Viable preservation the board incorporates measures to forestall infringement and territory annihilation inside safeguarded zones.

Feasible Land Use Arranging:

Incorporating standards of maintainable land use arranging can assist with limiting natural surroundings misfortune and fracture. This includes recognizing areas of high preservation esteem and focusing on them for assurance. Integrating green framework, drafting guidelines, and key advancement arranging can add to additional reasonable scenes.

Reclamation and Reforestation:

Rebuilding endeavors, including reforestation and natural surroundings restoration, can assist with neutralizing the effects of environment misfortune. Establishing local vegetation, reestablishing corrupted environments, and reconnecting divided territories are fundamental parts of preservation techniques. These drives frequently include local area commitment and the coordination of neighborhood information.

Local area Based Protection:

Drawing in neighborhood networks in preservation endeavors is essential for making long haul progress. Local area based protection includes enabling nearby partners, regarding customary information, and integrating native practices into land the executives systems. This approach cultivates a feeling of responsibility and stewardship, adjusting preservation objectives to the necessities and yearnings of networks.

Corporate and Government Responsibility:

Empowering corporate obligation and considering states responsible for manageable advancement rehearses are fundamental parts of natural surroundings preservation. Executing and implementing guidelines against territory annihilation, advancing capable asset extraction, and boosting harmless to the ecosystem rehearses add to relieving environment misfortune.

Training and Mindfulness:

Schooling and mindfulness building drives assume a urgent part in collecting public help for living space protection. Encouraging a comprehension of the natural significance of flawless living spaces, the results of fracture, and the potential arrangements engages people and networks to go with educated decisions in favor regarding biodiversity.

Contextual analyses:

Yellowstone to Yukon Preservation Drive:

The Yellowstone to Yukon Preservation Drive (Y2Y) is a cooperative exertion pointed toward keeping up with and reestablishing untamed life passageways across the North American Rough Mountains.

By associating safeguarded regions and working with the development of species like wild bears and wolves, Y2Y tends to the difficulties presented by natural surroundings discontinuity in this environmentally huge locale.

The Incomparable Eastern Reaches Drive, Australia:

Australia's Incredible Eastern Reaches Drive centers around monitoring and reestablishing territories along the east shoreline of the mainland. By stressing scene network, living space reclamation, and local area inclusion, the drive plans to address the dangers presented by natural surroundings misfortune and discontinuity to a different scope of animal groups, including marsupials and birds.

Agroforestry in Costa Rica:

Costa Rica has carried out agroforestry rehearses as a methodology to accommodate farming exercises with biodiversity protection. Agroforestry frameworks integrate trees into farming scenes, giving living space to natural life while supporting manageable agribusiness. This approach mitigates territory misfortune and discontinuity related with customary cultivating rehearses.

2.2 Effects on Wildlife Migration

Untamed life movement is a momentous normal peculiarity, fundamental for the endurance and environmental equilibrium of various species. It includes the occasional development of creatures between various environments, driven by different factors like environment, asset accessibility, and regenerative necessities. Nonetheless, human-prompted changes in scenes, including living space misfortune, discontinuity, and environmental change, present huge difficulties to untamed life relocation. This investigation digs into the impacts of these natural modifications on untamed life relocation, analyzing the ramifications for species elements, environment wellbeing, and the potential moderation systems to protect this basic biological interaction.

The Meaning of Natural life Relocation:

Environment Elements:

Natural life relocation is indispensable to environment elements, affecting supplement cycling, seed dispersal, and hunter prey collaborations. Transitory species assume key parts in keeping up with the wellbeing and working of different biological systems. For instance, the movement of herbivores can forestall overgrazing in specific regions, while hunters add to directing prey populaces.

Hereditary Variety:

Movement takes into consideration the blending of hereditarily different populaces, upgrading the general strength and versatility of species. Hereditary variety is significant for populaces to adapt to ecological changes, sicknesses, and different difficulties.

Transitory ways of behaving add to the quality stream between various gatherings, keeping a solid and hearty hereditary pool.

Biodiversity Protection:

Numerous transient species are cornerstone or umbrella species, meaning their protection helps a great many different animal types in their environments. Safeguarding transitory courses and territories guarantees the protection of biodiversity and adds to the general soundness of environments. Transitory passageways frequently support a rich cluster of greenery, putting forth them central focuses for preservation attempts.

Financial and Social Importance:

Natural life relocation likewise holds monetary and social importance for some networks. Manageable the travel industry based on untamed life relocation can give financial open doors while encouraging a feeling of association and stewardship among nearby populaces. Moreover, transitory species frequently hold social significance in native and neighborhood customs, shaping a necessary piece of social legacy.

Effect of Environment Misfortune on Untamed life Relocation:

Fracture of Environments:

Environment misfortune, frequently determined by urbanization, farming, and foundation improvement, prompts the discontinuity of once-ceaseless scenes. This discontinuity makes hindrances that obstruct the normal development of natural life. For transitory species, divided territories bring about segregated populaces, upsetting conventional movement courses and restricting admittance to basic assets.

Loss of Visit Locales:

Numerous transient species depend on unambiguous visit destinations during their excursions to rest, feed, and refuel. Territory misfortune can bring about the debasement or complete vanishing of these critical visit locales. This misfortune thwarts the capacity of transient species to renew energy stores, improving the probability of fatigue and diminishing their possibilities of effective relocation.

Adjusted Scenes:

The change of scenes because of natural surroundings misfortune can establish novel conditions that may not be appropriate for specific transient species. For instance, the change of normal meadows into monoculture harvests can disturb the transitory courses of herbivores, prompting clashes with human exercises and possibly imperiling these species.

Expanded Human-Natural life Struggle:

Living space misfortune can carry transitory species into closer nearness to human settlements, expanding the potential for clashes. Creatures compelled to go amiss from their customary movement courses might enter regions where they face dangers like environment discontinuity, street mortality, or experiences with tamed creatures. This dynamic can prompt adverse results for both untamed life and human networks.

Impacts of Environmental Change on Natural life Movement:

Changes in Timing and Courses:

Environmental change can modify the timing and courses of natural life movement. Changes in temperature and precipitation designs impact the accessibility of food assets and trigger changes in the planning of occasional occasions, like blossoming and bug rise. Transitory species might have to change their relocation examples to synchronize with these changing biological signs.

Evolving Territories:

The warming environment can prompt changes in vegetation zones and modify the conveyance of territories along relocation courses. For instance, Icy biological systems are encountering quick changes because of environment warming, influencing the transient examples of species like caribou and Cold birds. These progressions can result in confuses between the planning of relocation and the accessibility of reasonable natural surroundings.

Rising Ocean Levels:

Waterfront and marine species, including numerous transitory fish and ocean turtles, are powerless against rising ocean levels brought about by environmental change. Waterfront natural surroundings critical for taking care of, reproducing, and settling might be lowered or debased, influencing the outcome of movement. Immersion of settling locales can bring about the deficiency of whole ages for species, for example, ocean turtles.

Outrageous Climate Occasions:

Environmental change adds to the expanded recurrence and force of outrageous climate occasions like typhoons, dry spells, and out of control fires. These occasions can upset movement courses, annihilate territories, and posture direct dangers to transient species. For example, extreme tempests can prompt mortality and living space annihilation for birds undertaking significant distance relocations.

Relief Techniques and Protection Approaches:

Safeguarded Halls:

Laying out and keeping up with safeguarded halls is a critical methodology for relieving the effects of environment misfortune and discontinuity on natural life relocation. These halls act as connective pathways between divided environments, taking into consideration the development of species. Safeguarded halls are frequently assigned and figured out how to guarantee the protection of basic movement courses.

Living space Reclamation:

Territory reclamation drives plan to turn around the effects of environment misfortune by replanting local vegetation, reestablishing debased biological systems, and working on the general nature of living spaces along movement courses. Connecting with nearby networks in rebuilding projects improves the odds of coming out on top and advances a feeling of shared liability regarding protection.

Environment Tough Protection Arranging:

Protection techniques should adjust to the changing environment by integrating environment versatile preparation. This includes distinguishing and safeguarding natural surroundings that are supposed to stay reasonable for transient species under future environment situations. Environment strong protection arranging considers the expected changes in species disseminations and movement designs.

Manageable Land Use Practices:

Empowering economical land use rehearses is fundamental for limiting natural surroundings misfortune and discontinuity. Carrying out measures, for example, agroforestry, capable logging, and eco-accommodating foundation improvement can assist with keeping up with biological network and backing natural life movement. Coordinated effort with landowners and partners is significant for the outcome of such drives.

Global Collaboration:

Numerous transient species navigate worldwide lines during their excursions. Viable protection, accordingly, requires worldwide collaboration and the advancement of transboundary preservation arrangements. Cooperative endeavors between nations can address shared difficulties, safeguard basic living spaces, and work with the administration of transient species across their whole reach.

Local area Commitment and Schooling:

Drawing in neighborhood networks in protection endeavors is fundamental for the drawn out progress of untamed life movement drives. Local area based preservation includes teaching occupants about the significance of transitory species, the dangers they face, and the job networks can play in their protection. Educated and drawn in networks are bound to help and partake in preservation endeavors.

Contextual investigations:

The Serengeti-Mara Biological system, Africa:

The Serengeti-Mara biological system, spreading over Tanzania and Kenya, has one of the most famous untamed life relocations - the yearly development of wildebeest and different herbivores. Preservation endeavors in this area center around safeguarding the transitory courses, laying out natural life passageways, and drawing in neighborhood networks in economical land use practices to guarantee the proceeded with progress of this striking relocation.

Yellowstone Pronghorn Gazelle Movement, USA:

The pronghorn gazelle movement in the More prominent Yellowstone Biological system is the longest earthbound relocation in the touching US. Protection drives have designated the safeguarding of movement passages, including the formation of underpasses and fencing to lessen street mortality. Cooperation between government organizations, NGOs, and neighborhood networks has been instrumental in safeguarding this transient course.

Icy Tern Movement, Worldwide:

The Icy tern, a seabird with the longest movement of any known creature, makes a trip from the Icy to the Antarctic and back every year. Environmental change presents difficulties to the tern's relocation, influencing the accessibility of prey along its course. Preservation endeavors for the Icy tern include concentrating on its transitory examples, safeguarding key rearing locales, and supporting for worldwide environment activity.

Chapter 3

Ecosystem Services And Land Use Change

Environment benefits, the different advantages that people get from biological systems, are fundamental for supporting life on The planet. These administrations include provisioning administrations like food and water, directing administrations, for example, environment guideline and infectious prevention, supporting administrations like supplement cycles, and social administrations that add to our prosperity and personal satisfaction. Land use change, driven by human exercises and developing financial elements, significantly impacts the conveyance of environment administrations. This investigation dives into the unpredictable transaction between biological system administrations and land use change, analyzing the effects on biodiversity, water assets, environment guideline, and human prosperity. Moreover, it investigates methodologies for economical land utilize that offset human necessities with the safeguarding of fundamental biological system administrations.

Understanding Environment Administrations:

Provisioning Administrations:

Provisioning administrations incorporate the substantial advantages that environments give, including food, freshwater, wood, and restorative plants. The efficiency of biological systems, affected via land use rehearses, decides the amount and nature of these administrations. For example, agrarian development and deforestation can upgrade food creation yet may think twice about provisioning administrations and biodiversity.

Directing Administrations:

Directing administrations include the limit of biological systems to manage regular cycles and equilibrium environmental capabilities. Environment guideline, water sanitization, infectious prevention, and fertilization are instances of managing administrations. Land use change can upset these administrations; deforestation, for example, can impact nearby environments, modify water cycles, and effect the commonness of sicknesses.

Supporting Administrations:

Supporting administrations are principal to the development of other biological system administrations. They incorporate cycles like supplement cycling, soil development, and photosynthesis. Land use rehearses that debase soil quality, upset supplement cycles, or adjust essential efficiency can think twice about administrations, influencing the general strength and supportability of biological systems.

Social Administrations:

Social administrations are non-material advantages that add to human prosperity and social character. Tasteful encounters, profound and sporting qualities, and motivation drawn from nature fall under social administrations. Urbanization, contamination, and living space corruption coming about because of land use change can reduce social administrations, influencing the tasteful and profound associations individuals have with nature.

Effect of Land Use Change on Environment Administrations:

Biodiversity Misfortune:

Biodiversity misfortune is an immediate result of land use change, especially territory obliteration and fracture. Environments wealthy in biodiversity give a huge number of administrations, from bother control to fertilization. Land transformation for farming, urbanization, and framework advancement can prompt the deficiency of species, diminishing the strength and versatile limit of environments.

Water Assets:

Changes in land use have huge ramifications for water assets and hydrological cycles. Deforestation can adjust precipitation examples and increment spillover, prompting changes in stream and water accessibility. Agrarian practices, for example, water system and pesticide use, impact water quality. Economical land use rehearses are fundamental for protecting water assets and guaranteeing their proceeded with accessibility.

Environment Guideline:

Woods assume a critical part in environment guideline by sequestering carbon dioxide and controlling temperatures through evapotranspiration. Land use change, especially deforestation and transformation of normal scenes, adds to ozone harming substance discharges, worsening environmental change. Safeguarding carbon-rich environments and taking on manageable land use rehearses are basic for environment guideline.

Soil Wellbeing and Fruitfulness:

Land use change can prompt soil corruption, influencing its wellbeing and fruitfulness. Impractical agrarian practices, deforestation, and urbanization can bring about soil disintegration, supplement consumption, and loss of natural matter. Solid soils are fundamental for supporting plant development, supplement cycling, and water maintenance, featuring the significance of reasonable land the board.

Air and Water Quality:

Urbanization and modern exercises related with land use change can add to air and water contamination. Spillover from rural fields conveying composts and pesticides, as well as contaminations from metropolitan regions, can think twice about quality. Moreover, deforestation and changes in land cover can impact air quality, with suggestions for human wellbeing and biological system prosperity.

Techniques for Reasonable Land Use:

Agroecology and Manageable Horticulture:

Agroecology advances manageable and environmentally sound farming practices that focus on biodiversity, soil wellbeing, and asset effectiveness. Practices, for example, agroforestry, natural cultivating, and incorporated bug the board add to manageable land use by diminishing the ecological effect of farming while at the same time keeping up with or further developing yields.

Green Framework and Metropolitan Preparation:

Green framework coordinates normal components into metropolitan scenes, advancing biodiversity, relieving metropolitan intensity islands, and further developing air and water quality. Economical metropolitan arranging includes safeguarding green spaces, making parks, and consolidating nature-based answers for improve the versatility of metropolitan biological systems and offer social types of assistance to inhabitants.

Woodland Protection and Reforestation:

Woodland protection and reforestation endeavors are pivotal for safeguarding biodiversity, sequestering carbon, and controlling environment. Safeguarded regions, reasonable logging practices, and reforestation drives add to keeping up with or reestablishing backwoods biological systems, in this manner supporting a scope of environment administrations.

Watershed The executives:

Watershed the executives centers around protecting the strength of whole watersheds, taking into account the interconnectedness of land, water, and biological systems.

Practices like riparian cradle zones, feasible farming, and reforestation in basic watersheds add to keeping up with water quality, managing stream, and supporting oceanic environments.

Biological system Based Variation to Environmental Change:

Environment based transformation includes utilizing regular biological systems to assist networks with adjusting to the effects of environmental change. This incorporates safeguarding mangroves to safeguard against storm floods, keeping up with solid wetlands for flood control, and coordinating regular foundation into environment strength methodologies.

Installment for Biological system Administrations (PES):

Installment for Biological system Administrations is a monetary methodology that perceives the worth of environment benefits and remunerates landowners for their part in safeguarding these administrations. PES projects can give motivating forces to feasible land the executives rehearses, for example, keeping up with timberland cover or embracing protection farming.

Local area Based Preservation:

Connecting with nearby networks in protection endeavors is critical for the progress of economical land use drives. Local area based protection includes engaging neighborhood partners, regarding conventional information, and integrating native practices into land the board procedures. This approach cultivates a feeling of responsibility and stewardship, adjusting protection objectives to the necessities and yearnings of networks.

Contextual analyses:

Costa Rica's Installment for Biological system Administrations Program:

Costa Rica's PES program is a spearheading drive that remunerates landowners for the ecological administrations given by their woodlands. The program has effectively expanded timberland cover, protected biodiversity, and added to water asset preservation. It fills in as a model for integrating monetary motivators into preservation endeavors.

China's Slanting Area Change Program:

China's Slanting Area Change Program centers around changing over steeply inclining horticultural land into woods or meadows. This drive intends to battle soil disintegration, further develop water quality, and improve biodiversity. By incorporating biological system administrations into land use choices, China tends to ecological difficulties while advancing practical turn of events.

Metropolitan Greening in Singapore:

Singapore's metropolitan arranging integrates broad green spaces, parks, and vertical nurseries to improve the city-state's versatility and personal satisfaction. Metropolitan greening drives add to further developed air and water quality, support biodiversity, and give sporting spaces to occupants. Singapore shows the way that manageable land use practices can be coordinated into metropolitan turn of events.

3.1 Role of Ecosystem Services in Conservation

Protection endeavors are inherently connected to the administrations biological systems give, shaping a unique exchange between the conservation of biodiversity and the prosperity of human social orders. Biological system benefits, the advantages that nature offers to mankind, are essential for keeping up with environmental equilibrium, supporting different living things, and adding to the personal satisfaction for individuals all over the planet. This investigation digs into the complex job of biological system administrations in preservation, looking at how these administrations support biodiversity, impact environmental strength, and add to practical turn of events.

Characterizing Environment Administrations:

Environment administrations are classified into four principal types: provisioning, directing, supporting, and social administrations.

Provisioning Administrations:

Provisioning administrations incorporate the unmistakable products that environments give, including food, freshwater, wood, and restorative plants. These administrations are fundamental for meeting essential human necessities and supporting financial exercises. For example, woodlands add to the provisioning of lumber, non-wood timberland items, and water assets, while agrarian environments supply food yields and animals.

Controlling Administrations:

Controlling administrations include the limit of environments to manage normal cycles and equilibrium biological capabilities. Environment guideline, water purging, infectious prevention, and fertilization are instances of controlling administrations. Timberlands, wetlands, and seas assume basic parts in directing environment designs, purging water, controlling irritations, and supporting pollinators.

Supporting Administrations:

Supporting administrations are essential to the development of other biological system administrations. They incorporate cycles like supplement cycling, soil arrangement, and essential efficiency.

Solid soils, for instance, support plant development, supplement cycling, and water maintenance, in this way adding to the general versatility and maintainability of biological systems.

Social Administrations:

Social administrations are non-material advantages that add to human prosperity and social personality. Stylish encounters, profound and sporting qualities, and motivation drawn from nature fall under social administrations. Safeguarded normal regions, beautiful scenes, and biodiversity-rich conditions give social advantages that upgrade human personal satisfaction.

Environment Administrations and Biodiversity Protection:

Biodiversity as a Key Provisioning Administration:

Biodiversity, as a foundation of biological system administrations, supports many provisioning administrations. Different environments give a wide exhibit of assets fundamental for human endurance, including an assortment of food sources, restorative plants, and hereditary variety for crop reproducing. Biodiversity adds to the flexibility of biological systems, making them more versatile to natural changes.

Fertilization Administrations and Farming:

Biological system administrations, especially fertilization, assume a fundamental part in farming. Many harvests rely upon pollinators like honey bees, butterflies, and birds for propagation. The variety of pollinators guarantees the versatility of fertilization administrations, adding to trim yields and food security. Preservation endeavors that help pollinator natural surroundings contribute straightforwardly to the manageability of agribusiness.

Carbon Sequestration and Environment Guideline:

Woods and different biological systems assume a basic part in environment guideline by sequestering carbon dioxide, an ozone depleting substance liable for an Earth-wide temperature boost. The preservation of timberlands and the reclamation of corrupted environments add to carbon sequestration, moderating the effects of environmental change. Safeguarding these controlling administrations is basic for environment strength.

Water Decontamination and Amphibian Biodiversity:

Oceanic environments, like wetlands and mangroves, give water filtration administrations by separating toxins and keeping up with water quality. Biodiversity inside oceanic frameworks, including different fish species, adds to the harmony between environments and supports maintainable fisheries.

Preservation endeavors zeroed in on sea-going biodiversity add to the assurance of these fundamental administrations.

Infection Guideline and Biological system Wellbeing:

Environments give directing administrations that impact sickness elements. For instance, sound environments with different fauna can direct the predominance of illness vectors like mosquitoes. Biodiversity adds to the equilibrium of hunter prey connections, affecting the overflow of species that might go about as sickness repositories.

Biological system Flexibility and Protection:

Supporting Administrations and Biological system Flexibility:

Supporting administrations, like supplement cycling and soil arrangement, add to the general flexibility of biological systems. Biodiversity assumes a vital part in supporting these administrations, as various species add to the complicated snare of biological connections. The variety of plant species, for example, adds to supplement cycling and soil wellbeing, improving biological system flexibility to unsettling influences.

Controlling Administrations and Flexibility:

Directing administrations, including environment guideline and infectious prevention, impact the flexibility of biological systems to evolving conditions. Biodiversity upgrades the capacity of environments to adapt to unsettling influences like outrageous climate occasions, vermin, and sicknesses. Versatile biological systems are better prepared to recuperate from unsettling influences and keep up with their usefulness.

Social Administrations and Human Association with Nature:

Social administrations, which incorporate tasteful, sporting, and profound qualities got from nature, assume a part in encouraging human prosperity and emotional wellness. Individuals' association with nature, worked with by safeguarded regions, picturesque scenes, and biodiversity-rich conditions, adds to their general feeling of prosperity. Rationing these social administrations guarantees the conservation of this inborn human instinct association.

Difficulties to Environment Administrations and Preservation:

Living space Misfortune and Fracture:

Living space misfortune and fracture, frequently determined by urbanization, agribusiness, and framework advancement, present huge difficulties to the conveyance of biological system administrations. The transformation of regular natural surroundings into human-overwhelmed scenes can prompt the deficiency of biodiversity, disturbance of environmental cycles, and a decrease in the arrangement of administrations.

Environmental Change:

Environmental change addresses a significant danger to both biodiversity and the arrangement of biological system administrations. Changes in temperature, precipitation examples, and outrageous climate occasions can modify the dissemination of species, disturb biological cooperations, and effect the accessibility of administrations. Protection endeavors should consider environment strength to guarantee the proceeded with conveyance of administrations.

Overexploitation of Assets:

Unreasonable double-dealing of normal assets, for example, overfishing, deforestation, and extreme utilization of freshwater, can drain biological systems and undermine their capacity to offer types of assistance. Preservation systems should address the maintainable administration of assets to guarantee their proceeded with accessibility.

Contamination and Debasement:

Contamination, including air and water contamination, also as soil debasement, can subvert the limit of biological systems to offer types of assistance. Toxins from rural spillover, modern releases, and ill-advised garbage removal can influence water quality, biodiversity, and the strength of biological systems. Protection endeavors should address contamination to shield environment administrations.

Protection Systems to Shield Environment Administrations:

Safeguarded Regions and Biodiversity Protection:

Laying out and really overseeing safeguarded regions is a foundation of biodiversity protection and the conservation of biological system administrations. Safeguarded regions give safe-havens to assorted species, add to the support of regular cycles, and proposition social and sporting advantages to networks.

Reasonable Land Use Practices:

Feasible land use rehearses, for example, agroecology, economical horticulture, and dependable ranger service, add to the safeguarding of environment administrations. Rehearses that limit territory obliteration, keep up with soil wellbeing, and advance biodiversity-accommodating methodologies guarantee the proceeded with arrangement of provisioning, managing, supporting, and social administrations.

Biological system Reclamation and Reforestation:

Biological system reclamation drives, including reforestation and territory rebuilding, add to the recuperation of corrupted environments. Reforestation, specifically, upgrades carbon sequestration, upholds biodiversity, and reestablishes directing administrations. Reclamation endeavors are fundamental for revamping biological system wellbeing and flexibility.

Local area Commitment and Reasonable Turn of events:

Drawing in neighborhood networks in preservation endeavors is critical for the progress of drives pointed toward safeguarding biological system administrations. Local area based protection approaches include engaging nearby partners, coordinating conventional information, and encouraging a feeling of stewardship. Maintainable improvement rehearses that focus on both human requirements and biological manageability add to long haul preservation objectives.

Incorporated Scene The executives:

Incorporated scene the executives includes arranging and overseeing scenes to adjust protection and improvement objectives. This approach thinks about the interconnectedness of biological systems, human exercises, and the conveyance of environment administrations. Incorporated scene the executives looks to advance land use to serve both biodiversity and human prosperity.

Contextual investigations:

Costa Rican Installment for Environment Administrations Program:

Costa Rica's Installment for Biological system Administrations (PES) program is a spearheading drive that remunerates landowners for rationing backwoods and giving environment administrations like carbon sequestration and water guideline. The program has effectively added to backwoods protection, supportable land use, and the conservation of fundamental administrations.

Agroforestry Practices in Ethiopia:

Agroforestry rehearses in Ethiopia include coordinating trees into rural scenes, giving various advantages like superior soil ripeness, expanded water maintenance, and broadened pay hotspots for ranchers. These practices add to supporting administrations, improving versatility, and encouraging maintainable land use.

Yakushima World Legacy Site, Japan:

The Yakushima World Legacy Site in Japan is perceived for its rich biodiversity and antiquated timberlands. Protection endeavors in Yakushima center around safeguarding the one of a kind verdure, directing administrations like carbon sequestration, and offering social types of assistance through eco-the travel industry. The site embodies the mix of protection with social and natural qualities.

3.2 Consequences of Altered Landscapes

The change of scenes, driven by human exercises like urbanization, agribusiness, and framework improvement, has significant outcomes on environments, biodiversity, and the prosperity of both human and non-human occupants. As normal natural surroundings are changed and divided, a fountain of natural, social, and biological effects follows. This investigation dives into the results of modified scenes, analyzing the expansive impacts on biological systems, biodiversity, water assets, and the unpredictable harmony between human turn of events and ecological maintainability.

Ecological Effects:

Natural surroundings Annihilation:

Adjusted scenes frequently bring about the by and large obliteration of normal territories. Deforestation, metropolitan extension, and modern exercises lead to the deficiency of basic biological systems like timberlands, wetlands, and meadows. The obliteration of environments disturbs the unpredictable snare of life, prompting the decay or loss of plant and creature species.

Biodiversity Misfortune:

Territory change is an essential driver of biodiversity misfortune. As normal scenes are changed, species adjusted to explicit biological specialties face difficulties in endurance. Divided living spaces seclude populaces, diminishing hereditary variety and expanding the weakness of species to ecological changes. The combined impact is a deficiency of biodiversity, with potential flowing effects on environment working.

Soil Corruption:

Changes in land use works on, including agribusiness and deforestation, add to soil debasement. Soil disintegration, loss of fruitfulness, and expanded weakness to dry season are normal outcomes. Debased soils influence rural efficiency, compromise water quality, and decrease the capacity of biological systems to help plant and microbial life.

Social Effects:

Dislodging and Migration:

Urbanization and huge scope foundation projects frequently bring about the uprooting of human populaces. Networks living in regions reserved for advancement might be compelled to move, prompting social disturbance, loss of livelihoods, and difficulties in keeping up with social characters. The social texture of uprooted networks can be significantly affected by changed scenes.

Asset Shortage and Struggle:

Modified scenes add to asset shortage, particularly in districts where normal assets are widely taken advantage of. Contest for water, arable land, and other fundamental assets can prompt struggles among networks or even countries. Ecological debasement escalates asset shortage, compounding social pressures and possibly bringing about long haul clashes.

Influence on Jobs:

Changes in land use practices can have direct results on the jobs of networks subject to normal assets. For instance, deforestation for horticulture or logging may adversely affect nearby economies that depend on woods items. Reasonable land use rehearses are fundamental for guaranteeing the drawn out feasibility of livelihoods connected to the land.

Environmental Effects:

Adjusted Biological system Elements:

The change of scenes upsets laid out biological system elements. Changes in vegetation cover, water stream, and supplement cycles impact the associations among species and the accessibility of assets. Modified biological system elements can prompt the multiplication of obtrusive species, changes in fire systems, and a decrease in the general strength of environments.

Loss of Network:

Living space fracture coming about because of adjusted scenes decreases network between biological systems. Natural life halls are upset, hindering the development of species and restricting hereditary trade. The deficiency of network can prompt disconnected populaces, making species more vulnerable to infections, hereditary issues, and the effects of environmental change.

Water Asset Effects:

Changes in land use influence water assets by modifying regular hydrological cycles. Urbanization, deforestation, and farming practices can prompt expanded spillover, changes in stream, and the debasement of water quality. These effects have broad results on amphibian environments, influencing fish populaces, water-subordinate species, and in general biological system wellbeing.

Moderation and Economical Practices:

Biological system Reclamation:

Biological system reclamation drives assume a urgent part in relieving the results of modified scenes. Reestablishing debased natural surroundings, replanting local vegetation, and once again introducing species add to the recuperation of biological systems. Reclamation endeavors expect to upgrade biodiversity, further develop biological system benefits, and reestablish the regular equilibrium of scenes.

Reasonable Land Use Arranging:

Reasonable land use arranging includes offsetting human advancement with the conservation of biological systems. It incorporates techniques like green framework, shrewd metropolitan preparation, and coordinated scene the executives. By taking into account the natural worth of scenes, practical land use arranging looks to limit adverse consequences on the climate and keep up with the usefulness of biological systems.

Local area Commitment and Protection:

Drawing in nearby networks in protection endeavors is fundamental for tending to the social effects of adjusted scenes. Local area based protection approaches include teaming up with inhabitants, regarding conventional information, and integrating nearby points of view into land use choices. Preservation drives are bound to succeed when they line up with the necessities and desires of networks.

3.3 Assessing and Valuing Ecosystem Services

Evaluating and esteeming biological system administrations is a basic part of understanding the advantages that nature gives to humankind and the climate. Biological system administrations, enveloping provisioning, managing, supporting, and social administrations, assume an imperative part in supporting life on The planet. This investigation dives into the strategies and meaning of surveying and esteeming biological system administrations, revealing insight into how these methodologies add to informed independent direction, economical land the executives, and the protection of biodiversity.

Techniques for Surveying Environment Administrations:

Planning and Remote Detecting:

Planning and remote detecting advancements give important instruments to surveying environment administrations. Satellite symbolism and GIS (Geographic Data Framework) planning permit specialists to envision land cover changes, recognize areas of high biodiversity, and screen biological systems over the long run. These techniques help in understanding the spatial appropriation of administrations and their progressions because of human exercises or normal cycles.

Environmental Pointers:

Environmental pointers are measurements used to evaluate the wellbeing and working of biological systems. Biodiversity records, water quality boundaries, and soil wellbeing pointers are instances of apparatuses that assist with estimating the situation with biological systems. These markers give quantitative information, empowering specialists to assess the effect of land use changes on the arrangement of environment administrations.

Financial Valuation:

Financial valuation allots money related values to environment administrations, making their commitments unmistakable in monetary terms. Strategies like money saving advantage investigation, contingent valuation, and market evaluating assist with assessing the financial worth of administrations. Monetary valuation gives a language that policymakers and partners can comprehend, working with the joining of biological system administrations into dynamic cycles.

Partner Commitment and Neighborhood Information:

Drawing in partners, including nearby networks and native gatherings, is significant for an exhaustive evaluation of biological system administrations. Nearby information contributes experiences into social administrations, customary asset use, and the meaning of scenes. Consolidating assorted viewpoints guarantees that the evaluation catches the full range of environment administrations applicable to various networks.

Meaning of Evaluating and Esteeming Biological system Administrations:

Informed Navigation:

Evaluating and esteeming biological system administrations give chiefs vital data for educated and maintainable land the executives. Understanding the compromises related with various land use situations permits policymakers to pursue choices that offset monetary improvement with the protection of fundamental biological capabilities.

Preservation Arranging:

Preservation arranging benefits essentially from environment administration appraisals. Distinguishing areas of high biodiversity, basic water provisioning, or carbon sequestration focuses on locales for preservation endeavors. These appraisals guide the formation of safeguarded regions, rebuilding drives, and feasible land use practices to defend biological system administrations.

Reasonable Asset The executives:

For enterprises dependent on regular assets, for example, farming or ranger service, surveying biological system administrations is fundamental for maintainable asset the board. By evaluating the advantages given by biological systems, these businesses can take on rehearses that keep up with or improve the arrangement of administrations while limiting adverse consequences on biodiversity and environment wellbeing.

Environmental Change Moderation and Transformation:

Biological system administration evaluations add to environmental change alleviation and transformation procedures. Backwoods, wetlands, and different environments assume basic parts in sequestering carbon, managing water cycles, and giving flexibility against outrageous climate occasions. Understanding these administrations helps with planning methodologies that improve environment commitments to environmental change moderation and variation.

Public Mindfulness and Instruction:

Evaluating and esteeming biological system administrations add to public mindfulness and instruction. Imparting the significance of nature's commitments to human prosperity encourages a feeling of ecological stewardship. Informed residents are bound to help preservation drives, supportable practices, and arrangements that safeguard biological systems.

Difficulties and Contemplations:

Interconnectedness of Biological system Administrations:

Biological system administrations are frequently interconnected, and changes in a single help might have flowing impacts on others. Evaluating and esteeming these administrations separately may neglect the intricacy of their associations. All encompassing methodologics that consider the cooperative energies and compromises between administrations give a more complete comprehension.

Social and Moral Qualities:

Not all biological system administrations can be effortlessly evaluated in financial terms. Social administrations, for instance, hold enormous worth however might challenge to communicate in financial terms. Evaluations should recognize and consolidate social and moral qualities, guaranteeing a more comprehensive portrayal of the different manners by which biological systems add to human prosperity.

Dynamic Nature of Biological systems:

Biological systems are dynamic and can go through fast changes because of regular cycles or human exercises. Appraisals need to represent the unique idea of biological systems and consolidate fleeting aspects to catch the changeability in the arrangement of administrations over the long run.

Contextual investigations:

TEEB (The Financial matters of Environments and Biodiversity):

TEEB is a worldwide drive that spotlights on the monetary parts of biodiversity and environment administrations. TEEB appraisals give experiences into the monetary upsides of different administrations, including fertilization, water decontamination, and environment guideline. The drive underlines the mix of environment administration values into dynamic cycles at different levels.

Thousand years Biological system Appraisal (MEA):

The MEA, directed somewhere in the range of 2001 and 2005, was a historic drive surveying the outcomes of environment change for human prosperity. It gave a complete combination of the status and patterns of environment benefits worldwide. The MEA featured the significance of environments for human endurance and impacted global arrangement conversations on supportable turn of events.

Chapter 4

Conservation Strategies In The Face Of Land Use Change

Land use change, driven by extending human populaces, urbanization, and rural heightening, presents critical difficulties to biodiversity and biological system well-being. As regular scenes are changed, it becomes basic to create and execute viable preservation procedures that address the effects of land use change while advancing maintainable turn of events. This investigation dives into a thorough outline of protection procedures despite land use change, looking at the multi-layered approaches that offset human necessities with the conservation of natural honesty.

Understanding Area Use Change:

Definition and Drivers:

Land use change alludes to modifications in the manner land is used, frequently including shifts starting with one land cover type then onto the next. Normal drivers of land use change incorporate urbanization, rural extension, foundation advancement, and modern exercises. The elements of land use change differ territorially and are impacted by financial, political, and natural variables.

Kinds of Land Use Change:

Land use change can appear in different structures, including transformation of normal environments to horticultural land, deforestation, never-ending suburbia, and changes in water use designs. Each sort of land use change has extraordinary natural ramifications, influencing biodiversity, biological system administrations, and the general strength of environments.

Preservation Systems:

Safeguarded Regions and Biodiversity Preservation:

Laying out and successfully overseeing safeguarded regions is a key methodology for biodiversity protection even with land use change. Safeguarded regions act as safe-havens for different species, protecting basic territories from direct human effects. The formation of a very much associated organization of safeguarded regions keeps up with biological cycles and supports the development of species across scenes.

Hall Preservation and Availability:

Hall preservation includes protecting or reestablishing normal passageways that interface divided territories. These environmental hallways empower the development of species between segregated patches of territory, advancing hereditary variety and improving strength. Network is fundamental for tending to the adverse consequences of natural surroundings fracture brought about by different types of land use change.

Maintainable Land Use Arranging:

Incorporating protection objectives into land use arranging is fundamental for accomplishing a harmony between human turn of events and biological conservation. Reasonable land use arranging includes drafting regions for explicit purposes, executing green framework, and integrating natural contemplations into metropolitan and rustic turn of events. This approach means to limit the natural impression of human exercises.

Agroecology and Feasible Farming:

Agroecology advances environmentally manageable horticultural practices that focus on biodiversity, soil wellbeing, and asset effectiveness. Feasible agribusiness limits the ecological effect of cultivating exercises, underlines natural practices, and coordinates biodiversity-accommodating methodologies. By embracing agroecological standards, land use change as agribusiness can exist together with biodiversity protection.

Installment for Environment Administrations (PES):

PES programs give financial motivations to landowners to keeping up with or reestablishing biological system administrations. This approach perceives the worth of nature's commitments to human prosperity and intends to incorporate the outside advantages of biological systems. Installments might be coordinated towards rehearses that sequester carbon, protect water quality, or keep up with biodiversity, making financial motivations for feasible land the executives.

Environment Based Variation to Environmental Change:

Biological system based transformation includes utilizing regular environments to assist networks with adjusting to the effects of environmental change. Saving mangroves for storm flood assurance, keeping up with sound wetlands for flood control, and incorporating regular framework into environment versatility methodologies add to both environment variation and biodiversity protection.

Local area Based Protection:

Connecting with nearby networks in protection endeavors is essential for the outcome of drives despite land use change. Local area based preservation includes engaging nearby partners, regarding conventional information, and integrating native practices into land the executives procedures. This approach cultivates a feeling of responsibility and stewardship, adjusting preservation objectives to the requirements and desires of networks.

Contextual investigations:

Yasuní Public Park, Ecuador:

Yasuní Public Park in Ecuador is an illustration of a safeguarded region that has earned worldwide respect for its high biodiversity. The recreation area is arranged in the Amazon rainforest and appearances dangers from oil extraction and deforestation. Preservation endeavors in Yasuní include laying out safeguarded zones, drawing in with neighborhood networks, and looking for worldwide help to forestall oil investigation inside the recreation area.

The Green Belt and Street Drive (BRI) in China:

China's BRI, an aggressive framework and advancement project spreading over different nations, has ecological ramifications because of its expected effect ashore use. China has perceived the significance of maintainable advancement inside the BRI structure and is chipping away at consolidating green foundation, eco-accommodating innovations, and biodiversity protection measures into the drive. The point is to offset monetary advancement with ecological manageability.

Difficulties and Contemplations:

Strategy and Administration:

Compelling preservation procedures require strong strategies and hearty administration systems. Challenges frequently emerge when approaches favor momentary monetary increases over long haul natural manageability. Reinforcing natural guidelines, guaranteeing requirement, and advancing incorporated land use arranging are fundamental for conquering administration challenges.

Struggle Among Protection and Improvement Objectives:

Offsetting protection objectives with the formative necessities of developing populaces is a diligent test. Contending interests frequently lead to clashes, especially in districts where land is a limited asset. Incorporated approaches that consider both preservation and advancement targets are fundamental for tracking down economical arrangements.

Absence of Mindfulness and Training:

At times, the difficulties of land use change come from an absence of mindfulness and understanding among partners. Instructing people group, policymakers, and enterprises about the significance of biodiversity, environment administrations, and reasonable land use rehearses is vital for building support for preservation endeavors.

4.1 Adaptive Management Approaches

Versatile administration is a dynamic and adaptable way to deal with protection that recognizes the innate vulnerabilities in complex biological frameworks. Notwithstanding always changing ecological circumstances, versatile administration techniques permit preservation professionals to answer new data, unforeseen difficulties, and advancing social elements. This investigation digs into the standards, procedures, and contextual analyses of versatile administration draws near, featuring their importance in encouraging strength, advancing learning, and guaranteeing the drawn out progress of protection drives.

Standards of Versatile Administration:

Iterative Direction:

Versatile administration is described by an iterative dynamic interaction that includes persistent patterns of arranging, execution, checking, and learning. Each cycle adds to refining procedures in light of the criticism and bits of knowledge acquired from the past stages. This iterative nature permits protection specialists to adjust their methodologies in light of evolving conditions.

Adaptability and Trial and error:

Adaptability and an eagerness to explore are basic standards of versatile administration. Preservation procedures are treated as speculations that are tried through on-the-ground activities. By embracing trial and error, experts can evaluate the adequacy of various methodologies and change their techniques in view of noticed results.

Observing and Assessment:

Thorough checking and assessment are necessary parts of versatile administration. Information assortment and investigation give bits of knowledge into the environmental reactions to protection intercessions, permitting specialists to survey whether goals are being met. Observing additionally distinguishes surprising results, giving significant data to versatile direction.

Learning and Information Sharing:

Learning is a focal principle of versatile administration. The interaction includes gaining from triumphs as well as from disappointments and unforeseen results. Information dividing between partners, including researchers, neighborhood networks, and policymakers, cultivates a cooperative way to deal with protection. Versatile administration energizes open correspondence and the trading of different viewpoints.

Procedures of Versatile Administration:

Organized Independent direction:

Organized navigation is a technique utilized in versatile administration to assess elective preservation methodologies methodicallly. It includes recognizing the board goals, taking into account different choice other options, and surveying the compromises related with every choice. This approach assists protection specialists with pursuing informed choices in view of an exhaustive comprehension of expected results.

Situation Arranging:

Situation arranging includes creating conceivable future situations to investigate a scope of possible results and vulnerabilities. Preservation experts use situation wanting to expect and get ready for various environmental and social directions. By taking into account different situations, versatile administration techniques can be intended to be strong and adaptable despite assorted future circumstances.

Demonstrating and Reproduction:

Numerical models and recreation devices are significant for reenacting environment elements, anticipating the effects of mediations, and investigating expected future situations. Models assist traditionalists with testing speculations, figure out complex natural cycles, and survey the probable results of various administration techniques. Displaying upgrades the logical reason for dynamic in versatile administration.

Contextual investigations of Versatile Administration:

The Everglades Reclamation Venture, USA:

The Everglades Reclamation Venture is one of the biggest and most complex biological system rebuilding drives around the world. The venture expects to reestablish the normal hydrological examples of the Everglades environment in Florida. Versatile administration is a center part, with persistent checking, trial and error, and learning. The rebuilding endeavors include changing water stream, overseeing obtrusive species, and tending to supplement contamination in view of the bits of knowledge acquired from progressing versatile administration cycles.

The Incomparable Obstruction Reef Marine Park, Australia:

The Incomparable Obstruction Reef Marine Park is confronting numerous dangers, including coral blanching, contamination, and overfishing. Versatile administration is utilized to address these difficulties. The Reef 2050 Long haul Manageability Plan uses versatile administration standards to change preservation systems in light of new logical discoveries and arising dangers. Methodologies incorporate spatial drafting, fisheries the board, and endeavors to further develop water quality.

Meaning of Versatile Administration in Preservation:

Cultivating Strength:

Versatile administration adds to the strength of biological systems by considering changes in light of aggravations or evolving conditions. Versatile biological systems can more readily endure and recuperate from natural stressors, guaranteeing the steadiness of biodiversity and the arrangement of environment administrations.

Tending to Vulnerability:

Preservation endeavors work in innately questionable conditions, with natural frameworks impacted by powerful and frequently erratic variables. Versatile administration recognizes this vulnerability and gives an organized way to deal with pursuing choices despite inadequate data. It takes into account course rectifications as additional information opens up or as new difficulties emerge.

Gaining from Disappointment:

Disappointments are unavoidable in complex protection tries. What recognizes versatile administration is its accentuation on gaining from disappointments. Rather than survey difficulties as deterrents, specialists treat them as any open doors to refine procedures and upgrade the comprehension of biological frameworks. This learning-driven approach cultivates a culture of persistent improvement.

Powerful Partner Commitment:

Versatile administration empowers the association of assorted partners, including neighborhood networks, researchers, policymakers, and non-legislative associations. The commitment of partners in the dynamic cycle improves the adequacy of preservation methodologies. It guarantees that nearby information is thought of, and the social elements of protection are coordinated into versatile administration plans.

Long haul Practicality of Preservation Drives:

Versatile administration adds to the drawn out practicality of preservation drives by advancing dynamic and responsive systems. Rather than static administration designs that might become obsolete, versatile methodologies guarantee that preservation endeavors stay important and successful despite advancing environmental and cultural circumstances.

Difficulties and Contemplations:

Asset and Time Limitations:

Executing versatile administration requires assets for observing, information assortment, and examination. Restricted subsidizing and time limitations can ruin the complete utilization of versatile administration, especially in huge scope protection projects. Defeating these difficulties might require imaginative financing components and long haul responsibilities.

Protection from Change:

Versatile administration requires a readiness to head in a different direction in view of new data, which can be met with opposition from partners acquainted with customary protection draws near. Defeating protection from change includes viable correspondence, building trust, and showing the advantages of versatile administration in accomplishing preservation targets.

Information Holes and Logical Vulnerability:

Now and again, information holes and logical vulnerability might restrict the viability of versatile administration. Deficient comprehension of biological cycles or inadequate observing information can present difficulties. Versatile administration approaches should be intended to oblige vulnerability and focus on activities that upgrade information over the long haul.

Future Bearings and Amazing open doors:

Headways in Innovation:

Innovative headways, including remote detecting, sensor organizations, and information examination, present chances to upgrade the viability of versatile administration. These apparatuses empower more productive and thorough observing, giving constant information to illuminate independent direction.

Coordination with Conventional Natural Information:

Coordinating conventional natural information from nearby networks with logical methodologies improves the extensiveness of versatile administration.

Native points of view and practices contribute significant experiences into biological system elements, biodiversity, and the effects of land use change.

Worldwide Coordinated effort and Information Sharing:

The worldwide idea of numerous ecological difficulties highlights the significance of cooperation and information sharing. Protection professionals can profit from sharing encounters, examples learned, and best practices across locales and environments. Worldwide cooperation improves the versatile limit of preservation endeavors.

4.2 Sustainable Land Use Planning

Practical land use arranging is a visionary and coordinated approach that tries to orchestrate the contending requests ashore while shielding natural uprightness and advancing social and financial prosperity. Even with raising urbanization, rural extension, and modern turn of events, the requirement for maintainable land use arranging has never been more basic. This investigation digs into the standards, techniques, difficulties, and contextual analyses of reasonable land use arranging, featuring its urgent job in accomplishing a harmony between human necessities and natural protection.

Standards of Practical Land Use Arranging:

Mix of Environmental and Social Objectives:

Feasible land use arranging requires the combination of biological and social objectives. It perceives that human prosperity is unpredictably connected to the strength of environments. Adjusting the requirement for improvement with the safeguarding of basic territories, biodiversity, and biological system administrations is principal to accomplishing maintainability.

Multi-Partner Commitment:

The contribution of different partners, including nearby networks, legislative bodies, NGOs, and confidential ventures, is a foundation of practical land use arranging. Drawing in partners guarantees that the arranging system consolidates different viewpoints, nearby information, and local area desires. This participatory methodology encourages possession and works with the execution of powerful plans.

Versatile Administration and Adaptability:

Maintainable land use arranging perceives the unique idea of biological systems and cultural requirements. Consolidating versatile administration standards considers adaptability in answering evolving conditions. Observing, criticism instruments, and occasional audits empower organizers to change systems in light of advancing information and arising difficulties.

Safeguarding of Green Spaces and Biodiversity:

Safeguarding green spaces, normal natural surroundings, and biodiversity areas of interest is a vital rule of supportable land use arranging. Perceiving the characteristic worth of biological systems, organizers intend to keep up with environmental passageways, safeguard imperiled species, and support biodiversity. Green spaces additionally add to sporting open doors, mental prosperity, and tasteful qualities for networks.

Procedures of Economical Land Use Arranging:

Drafting and Land Grouping:

Drafting includes ordering land into various zones in light of its reasonableness for different purposes. Private, business, modern, rural, and protection zones are normal characterizations. Practical land use arranging utilizes drafting to distribute regions for advancement while assigning spaces for ecological protection and sporting purposes.

Green Framework Arranging:

Green framework arranging underscores the joining of regular elements, like parks, backwoods, wetlands, and scenic routes, into the metropolitan and rustic scene. This approach improves biological system administrations, including air and water filtration, environment guideline, and biodiversity support. Green foundation adds to the general flexibility and manageability of land use.

Minimized and Blended Use Improvement:

Empowering reduced and blended use improvement designs limits endless suburbia and the change of normal territories. By advancing higher-thickness improvement, feasible land use arranging expects to decrease the biological impression of metropolitan regions, upgrade walkability, and enhance the utilization of framework and assets.

Environment Based Arranging:

Environment based arranging includes considering the natural elements of scenes in the arranging system. This approach recognizes and focuses on regions that give basic environment administrations, like water guideline, fertilization, and carbon sequestration. Environment based arranging tries to keep up with the wellbeing and usefulness of normal frameworks.

Contextual investigations of Reasonable Land Use Arranging:

Curitiba, Brazil:

Curitiba is many times refered to as a model for manageable metropolitan preparation. The city executed a thorough public transportation framework, focused on green spaces, and embraced drafting guidelines that support blended use improvement. These drives have prompted diminished gridlock, further developed air quality, and improved personal satisfaction for occupants.

Portland, Oregon, USA:

Portland has earned respect for its way to deal with reasonable land use arranging, zeroing in on metropolitan development limits, transportation arranging, and green structure rehearses. The city's obligation to saving regular regions, advancing public travel, and empowering maintainable structure configuration has added to an all the more harmless to the ecosystem and bearable metropolitan climate.

Difficulties and Contemplations:

Clashing Interests and Partner Debates:

Maintainable land use arranging frequently experiences difficulties connected with clashing interests among partners. Designers, tree huggers, and neighborhood networks might have dissimilar perspectives ashore use needs. Conquering these questions requires viable correspondence, intercession, and figuring out something worth agreeing on that lines up with maintainability objectives.

Momentary Financial Tensions:

Financial tensions for momentary additions can block practical land use arranging. Designers might focus on quick benefits over long haul supportability, prompting choices that compromise natural protection. Offsetting financial improvement with environmental manageability requires boosting economical practices and taking into account the drawn out advantages of protection.

Absence of Satisfactory Information and Exploration:

Deficient information and examination on biological frameworks and land use examples can obstruct the adequacy of maintainable land use arranging. Vigorous information on biodiversity, environment administrations, and land cover changes are fundamental for going with informed choices. Interests in exploration and observing are important to address this test.

Advantages and Open doors:

Environmental Change Relief and Transformation:

Reasonable land use arranging assumes an essential part in environmental change relief and variation. By protecting regular carbon sinks, like woodlands and wetlands, and advancing reasonable advancement rehearses, organizers add to lessening ozone depleting substance outflows and upgrading the versatility of networks to environment influences.

Upgraded Environment Administrations:

Focusing on practical land use prompts upgraded environment administrations. Green spaces and normal natural surroundings support fertilization, water cleaning, and sporting open doors. The conservation of biodiversity adds to the general soundness of biological systems and guarantees the coherence of fundamental administrations for human prosperity.

Tough and Decent People group:

Feasible land use arranging makes tough and bearable networks. Minimal turn of events, blended use drafting, and admittance to green spaces add to worked on personal satisfaction. Walkable areas, productive public transportation, and nearness to nature improve local area prosperity and decrease the ecological impression of metropolitan regions.

Future Headings and Advancements:

Innovation Coordination:

The coordination of innovation, including Geographic Data Framework (GIS) planning, remote detecting, and information examination, upgrades the accuracy and productivity of economical land use arranging. These apparatuses give ongoing information, spatial examination, and situation demonstrating, permitting organizers to pursue more educated choices.

Nature-Based Arrangements:

Nature-based arrangements include utilizing regular cycles and biological systems to address ecological difficulties. Practical land use arranging progressively integrates nature-based arrangements, like green rooftops, metropolitan woods, and normal water maintenance regions. These methodologies add to environment versatility, biodiversity preservation, and maintainable metropolitan turn of events.

Round Economy Standards:

Round economy standards advance asset effectiveness and waste decrease. Reasonable land use arranging can incorporate round economy ideas by focusing on brownfield redevelopment, reusing materials, and advancing supportable waste administration rehearses. These standards add to a more regenerative and supportable way to deal with improvement.

4.3 Restoration and Rehabilitation Initiatives

Reclamation and recovery drives are necessary parts of worldwide endeavors to address ecological debasement and biodiversity misfortune. Despite boundless environment obliteration, deforestation, and the effects of environmental change, these drives mean to recover and restore biological systems, encouraging flexibility and advancing maintainable conjunction among nature and human exercises. This investigation dives into the standards, techniques, advantages, and difficulties of reclamation and recovery drives, highlighting their importance chasing an additional practical and environmentally adjusted world.

Standards of Reclamation and Recovery:

Environment Based Approach:

Reclamation and recovery drives embrace a biological system based approach, perceiving the interconnectedness of species, living spaces, and natural cycles. Rather than zeroing in exclusively on individual species or parts, this all encompassing methodology means to reestablish whole environments, guaranteeing their usefulness and flexibility.

Local Species Usage:

The utilization of local species is an essential rule in rebuilding and restoration projects. Local plants and creatures are adjusted to nearby natural circumstances, upgrading their capacity to flourish and add to biological system working. Using local species additionally helps protect biodiversity and supports the re-foundation of normal living spaces.

Versatile Administration:

Versatile administration standards are utilized to explore the vulnerabilities inborn in rebuilding and restoration projects. This includes constant checking, gaining from the two triumphs and disappointments, and changing systems in view of developing information. Versatile administration guarantees that reclamation endeavors are receptive to changing natural circumstances.

Techniques of Rebuilding and Recovery:

Afforestation and Reforestation:

Afforestation includes establishing trees in regions that were not recently forested, while reforestation centers around replanting trees in regions that have been deforested. These drives add to carbon sequestration, soil adjustment, and the reclamation of basic environments for biodiversity.

Wetland Reclamation:

Wetland reclamation includes restoring or restoring wetland environments, including bogs, marshes, and mangroves. These regions assume a significant part in water filtration, flood control, and supporting different plant and creature species. Wetland rebuilding assists improve with watering quality and gives fundamental environment administrations.

Reclamation of Corrupted Rural Land:

Agrarian land corrupted by concentrated cultivating practices can be reestablished through maintainable land the board strategies. Carrying out agroecological standards, for example, cover trimming, crop revolution, and agroforestry, advances soil wellbeing, diminishes disintegration, and upgrades biodiversity in agrarian scenes.

Advantages of Reclamation and Recovery Drives:

Biodiversity Preservation:

One of the essential advantages of reclamation and recovery drives is the protection of biodiversity. By reestablishing normal living spaces, giving reasonable circumstances to local species, and tending to the effects of natural surroundings fracture, these drives add to the safeguarding of assorted biological systems.

Environmental Change Alleviation:

Reclamation endeavors, particularly afforestation and reforestation, assume a significant part in moderating environmental change. Woods go about as carbon sinks, engrossing and putting away carbon dioxide from the environment. Reforestation projects add to carbon sequestration, assisting with balancing ozone depleting substance outflows.

Environment Administrations Improvement:

Reclamation and recovery drives upgrade biological system benefits that are fundamental for human prosperity. Further developed water quality, expanded fertilization, and improved soil richness are instances of administrations that benefit the two biological systems and neighborhood networks.

Difficulties and Contemplations:

Fracture and Network:

Environment fracture represents a test to rebuilding drives, as disengaged patches of reestablished territory might restrict the development of species. Guaranteeing availability between reestablished regions is vital for advancing hereditary variety and permitting species to move and adjust to changing ecological circumstances.

Intrusive Species and Contest:

The presence of intrusive species can block reclamation endeavors by outcompeting local vegetation or going after neighborhood fauna. Overseeing obtrusive species and executing measures to control their spread are fundamental contemplations in rebuilding projects.

Asset Restrictions:

Reclamation and recovery drives frequently face asset impediments, including monetary imperatives and a deficiency of talented staff. Getting subsidizing, building organizations, and utilizing local area association can assist with conquering these difficulties and improve the viability of reclamation projects.

Examples of overcoming adversity and Contextual investigations:

Loess Level Watershed Restoration, China:

The Loess Level Watershed Restoration project in China is an enormous scope exertion pointed toward battling soil disintegration and further developing water maintenance in a locale inclined to desertification. Through afforestation, terracing, and soil preservation gauges, the task has effectively reestablished debased land, worked on neighborhood occupations, and upgraded environment administrations.

Yamuna Biodiversity Park, India:

The Yamuna Biodiversity Park in Delhi, India, is an eminent illustration of metropolitan reclamation. Based on a once debased floodplain, the recreation area utilizes local plant species to reestablish a different scope of living spaces. It fills in as a green lung for the city, advancing biodiversity protection and giving sporting spaces to the local area.

Chapter 5

Balancing Human Development And Conservation Objectives

The multifaceted dance between human turn of events and protection targets lies at the core of the worldwide test to accomplish maintainability. As the human populace develops, social orders urbanize, and economies grow, the tension on normal assets escalates, frequently prompting natural corruption, loss of biodiversity, and disturbance of environments. Finding some kind of harmony between addressing the necessities of a developing populace and protecting the planet's environmental respectability is a complicated errand that requests nuanced approaches, insightful strategies, and cooperative endeavors. This investigation dives into the complex elements of adjusting human turn of events and protection goals, inspecting the difficulties, standards, contextual investigations, and likely pathways toward an economical conjunction.

Challenges in Adjusting Human Turn of events and Preservation:

Populace Development and Urbanization:

The total populace proceeds to develop, and the pattern towards urbanization is speeding up. As additional individuals move to urban areas looking for valuable open doors, metropolitan extension infringes on regular living spaces, prompting environment misfortune, discontinuity, and expanded strain on biological systems.

Asset Extraction and Double-dealing:

Financial advancement frequently depends on the extraction and abuse of regular assets, including backwoods, minerals, and water. Unreasonable asset practices can prompt deforestation, soil corruption, and consumption of imperative environments, risking biodiversity and biological system administrations.

Framework Advancement:

Framework projects, like streets, dams, and metropolitan turns of events, can have huge natural effects. Modifying scenes for human requirements can disturb biological systems, section environments, and add to the decay of weak species.

Environmental Change and Ecological Corruption:

The interconnected difficulties of environmental change and ecological corruption further confuse the undertaking of adjusting advancement and protection.

Outrageous climate occasions, climbing temperatures, and changes in precipitation designs enhance the strain on biological systems and fuel existing weaknesses.

Standards for Adjusting Advancement and Preservation:

Economical Improvement Objectives (SDGs):

The Unified Countries' Supportable Improvement Objectives give a system to coordinating social, financial, and natural targets. Adjusting human turn of events and protection lines up with a few SDGs, including those connected with clean water and disinfection, reasonable and clean energy, feasible urban areas and networks, life ashore, and life underneath water.

Biological system Based Approaches:

Taking on environment based approaches includes perceiving the worth of whole biological systems and their administrations. As opposed to zeroing in exclusively on individual species or assets, this approach considers the interconnectedness of regular frameworks and expects to keep up with their wellbeing and flexibility.

Incorporated Land Use Arranging:

Incorporated land use arranging includes planning different land uses to streamline benefits while limiting adverse consequences. This approach looks to adjust agribusiness, metropolitan turn of events, preservation, and other land utilizes through smart drafting, green foundation arranging, and economical administration rehearses.

Local area Commitment and Strengthening:

Drawing in and engaging nearby networks is fundamental for fruitful protection and advancement drives. By including networks in dynamic cycles, taking into account neighborhood information, and tending to local area needs, projects are bound to be socially adequate, naturally feasible, and monetarily reasonable.

Contextual investigations Outlining Fruitful Difficult exercises:

Costa Rica's Spearheading Preservation Model:

Costa Rica stands apart as a trailblazer in adjusting improvement and preservation. The nation has carried out an Installment for Environment Administrations (PES) program, compensating landowners for safeguarding backwoods and giving fundamental biological system administrations. This drive has added to critical reforestation and biodiversity preservation while supporting rustic vocations.

Land-Water-Energy Nexus in Singapore:

Singapore epitomizes effective coordinated land use arranging through its way to deal with the land-water-energy nexus. Notwithstanding restricted land assets, the city-state has figured out how to accomplish economical improvement by enhancing land use for urbanization, water catchment, and sustainable power creation.

Methodologies for Adjusting Human Turn of events and Protection:

Green Foundation and Metropolitan Preparation:

Green foundation arranging in metropolitan regions includes coordinating normal highlights, like parks, green spaces, and metropolitan woodlands, into the assembled climate. This approach upgrades biodiversity, further develops air and water quality, and gives sporting spaces to inhabitants, advancing a better and more economical metropolitan environment.

Round Economy Standards:

Taking on roundabout economy standards includes limiting waste, advancing asset effectiveness, and encouraging reasonable utilization and creation designs. By focusing on reusing, diminishing waste age, and reusing materials, social orders can alleviate the natural effect of financial exercises.

Practical Farming and Agroecology:

Executing manageable horticulture practices and embracing agroecological standards can alleviate the ecological effect of food creation. Practices like natural cultivating, agroforestry, and regenerative farming focus on soil wellbeing, decrease substance information sources, and backing biodiversity.

Comprehensive and Fair Advancement Strategies:

Guaranteeing that advancement approaches are comprehensive and evenhanded is essential for adjusting human turn of events and protection. Arrangements that focus on civil rights, address monetary incongruities, and shield the privileges of underestimated networks add to maintainable advancement results.

Innovation and Development:

Saddling innovation and advancement can work with practical improvement while limiting natural effect. Headways in sustainable power, accuracy horticulture, and natural observing advances offer chances to decouple financial development from asset consumption.

The Job of Worldwide Participation:

Worldwide Natural Administration:

Reinforcing worldwide natural administration is fundamental for addressing transboundary challenges connected with protection and improvement. Peaceful accords, shows, and cooperative drives give systems to shared liability and composed activity.

Innovation Move and Limit Building:

Working with the exchange of harmless to the ecosystem innovations and building the limit of non-industrial countries are basic parts of worldwide collaboration. By sharing information and assets, the worldwide local area can uphold supportable advancement rehearses around the world.

Difficulties and Contemplations:

Strategy Execution and Requirement:

The fruitful execution and requirement of strategies that balance improvement and protection goals stay a test. Irregularities in strategy application, absence of implementation components, and contending interests can frustrate progress.

Transient Monetary Tensions:

Transient monetary tensions frequently focus on quick acquires over long haul supportability. Defeating this challenge requires moving the concentration towards manageable and versatile monetary models that consider the prosperity of the two individuals and the planet.

Social and Financial Setting:

Adjusting improvement and preservation should think about the social and financial setting of every area. Arrangements that are setting explicit, regard neighborhood esteems, and integrate customary information are bound to be acknowledged and effective.

5.1 Conflict Between Agriculture and Conservation

The contention among horticulture and preservation addresses a urgent test in the journey for practical turn of events. As the worldwide interest for food ascends pair with populace development, rural extension frequently infringes upon normal living spaces, prompting biodiversity misfortune, soil corruption, and other ecological effects. Finding some kind of harmony between meeting the world's nourishing necessities and protecting the planet's biological trustworthiness requires creative arrangements, insightful strategies, and cooperative endeavors.

This investigation digs into the diverse components of the contention among farming and preservation, inspecting the main drivers, challenges, expected techniques, and contextual analyses that offer bits of knowledge into a more reasonable concurrence.

Underlying drivers of the Contention:

Land Change and Environment Misfortune:

Farming extension every now and again includes the transformation of normal scenes into croplands. This cycle brings about environment misfortune for various plant and creature species, prompting decreases in biodiversity and disturbance of biological system capabilities.

Escalated Farming Practices:

Escalated cultivating rehearses, for example, monoculture, extreme utilization of agrochemicals, and motorization, add to ecological debasement. These practices frequently lead to soil disintegration, water contamination, and the consumption of fundamental environment administrations.

Water Asset The board:

Farming is a significant shopper of freshwater assets. Wasteful water the board, including unreasonable water system and water-serious yields, can prompt the exhaustion of water sources, influencing both sea-going environments and the accessibility of water for different areas.

Deforestation and Discontinuity:

To clear a path for farming, enormous areas of woods are much of the time cleared, prompting deforestation. The fracture of normal natural surroundings intensifies the difficulties looked by numerous species, limiting their development and diminishing generally biodiversity.

Challenges in Adjusting Farming and Preservation:

Clashing Area Use Needs:

The opposition for land between horticultural extension and protection targets represents a huge test. Concluding which regions ought to be devoted to horticulture and which ought to be safeguarded for preservation is many times a wellspring of contention and requires cautious preparation.

Influence on Biological system Administrations:

Horticulture's effect on environments can think twice about conveyance of fundamental administrations, like fertilization, water refinement, and nuisance control.

Interruptions to these administrations can have flowing consequences for both regular frameworks and agrarian efficiency.

Loss of Biodiversity:

Environment annihilation and fracture related with horticulture add to the deficiency of biodiversity. This not just influences the species straightforwardly affected by cultivating exercises yet additionally disturbs the perplexing trap of cooperations inside environments.

Soil Debasement and Loss of Prolific Land:

Escalated farming works on, including the utilization of compound composts and monoculture, can prompt soil corruption. The deficiency of prolific dirt lessens the land's ability to help farming in the long haul, adding to a pattern of declining efficiency.

Expected Procedures for Practical Concurrence:

Agroecology and Feasible Cultivating Practices:

Agroecology advances cultivating rehearses that focus on environmental supportability. Procedures, for example, agroforestry, crop enhancement, and natural cultivating intend to emulate regular biological systems, upgrading biodiversity, further developing soil wellbeing, and lessening the ecological effect of horticulture.

Accuracy Farming and Innovation Joining:

Accuracy farming includes utilizing innovation, including GPS, sensors, and information investigation, to improve asset use. By exactly overseeing information sources like water, composts, and pesticides, ranchers can increment productivity, limit natural effect, and decrease the generally biological impression of agribusiness.

Safeguarded Regions and Preservation Set-Asides:

Assigning safeguarded regions and protection set-asides helps shield basic territories and biodiversity. By decisively distinguishing regions for preservation, policymakers can adjust the requirement for rural creation with the basic of saving environments and their administrations.

Agroforestry and Practical Land Use Arranging:

Agroforestry incorporates trees and bushes into horticultural scenes. This approach gives various advantages, including further developed soil fruitfulness, expanded biodiversity, and improved strength to environmental change. Feasible land use arranging that consolidates agroforestry can upgrade the harmony between farming efficiency and preservation.

Contextual analyses Showing Fruitful Methodologies:

Costa Rica's Installment for Environment Administrations (PES) Program:

Costa Rica's PES program is a spearheading drive that remunerates landowners for saving woodlands and giving biological system administrations. By esteeming the ecological advantages of unblemished environments, the program has effectively added to both preservation and feasible agribusiness.

The Green Unrest in India:

India's Green Upset, while supporting agrarian efficiency, has additionally confronted ecological difficulties. Be that as it may, drives like the Arrangement of Rice Increase (SRI) advance more feasible cultivating rehearses. SRI centers around asset streamlining, decreasing water utilization, and upgrading soil wellbeing.

Methodologies for Relieving Clashes:

Incorporated Scene The executives:

Incorporated scene the board includes planning land use across various areas, including horticulture, protection, and metropolitan turn of events. This approach tries to streamline the advantages of each land use while limiting negative externalities, cultivating an agreeable concurrence.

Installment for Environment Administrations (PES) Projects:

PES programs, similar to the one in Costa Rica, can be extended to different areas. By remunerating landowners for the natural administrations given by flawless environments, these projects make monetary motivations for preservation and maintainable land the executives.

Local area Based Protection:

Including neighborhood networks in preservation endeavors can cultivate a feeling of pride and stewardship. Local area based preservation drives engage nearby occupants to partake in dynamic cycles and execute maintainable horticultural practices that line up with protection targets.

The Job of Strategy and Administration:

Vital Land Use Arranging:

States assume a critical part in executing key land use arranging that considers both rural and preservation needs. Drafting guidelines, safeguarded region assignments, and motivations for manageable practices add to a powerful and adjusted approach.

Motivation Systems for Manageable Horticulture:

State run administrations can execute motivator systems to urge ranchers to embrace manageable horticultural practices. This might incorporate endowments for agroecological techniques, tax cuts for protection situated land use, or monetary help for innovation reception.

Difficulties and Contemplations:

Monetary Tensions and Transient Objectives:

Financial tensions and momentary improvement objectives frequently focus on quick acquires over long haul supportability. States, organizations, and networks need to perceive the drawn out advantages of reasonable practices and put resources into a stronger and environmentally sound future.

Worldwide Stock Chains and Market Elements:

The elements of worldwide inventory chains can add to impractical rural practices. Tending to these difficulties requires global participation, straightforwardness in supply chains, and endeavors to advance feasible and moral obtaining rehearses.

Social Value and Livelihoods:

Adjusting farming and preservation should likewise think about friendly value and the vocations of those ward on agribusiness. Changing to additional feasible practices ought to be joined by measures that safeguard the interests of ranchers and networks

5.2 Urbanization and Infrastructure Challenges

Urbanization, set apart by the development and extension of urban communities, is a characterizing pattern of the 21st hundred years. While metropolitan regions offer monetary open doors, social lavishness, and worked on expectations for everyday comforts, the related difficulties of quick urbanization and framework improvement can't be neglected. From overseeing populace development to guaranteeing economical foundation, urban communities all over the planet face complex issues that require cautious preparation, imaginative arrangements, and a promise to natural supportability. This investigation dives into the complex components of urbanization and the difficulties presented by foundation advancement, analyzing underlying drivers, likely methodologies, and contextual analyses that shed light on the way toward reasonable metropolitan development.

Chapter 6

Policy Frameworks For Land Use And Conservation

Despite heightening area use changes and the basic to save biodiversity, strong strategy systems assume an essential part in molding feasible turn of events. The test lies in creating strategies that balance the requirements of human social orders for financial development with the basic of defending biological systems and biodiversity. This investigation dives into the complicated universe of strategy structures for land use and preservation, analyzing the key parts, difficulties, triumphs, and expected roads for development in directing human-climate cooperations.

Grasping the Parts of Strategy Structures:

Drafting and Land Use Arranging:

At the center of successful land use and protection strategies lies exhaustive drafting and land use arranging. This includes sorting regions for different purposes, for example, private, business, horticultural, and preservation. Key land use arranging forestalls indiscriminate turn of events, limits natural effect, and jelly basic environments.

Safeguarded Regions and Protection Stores:

Laying out safeguarded regions and preservation holds is a foundation of protection strategies. These regions are assigned to protect biological systems, biodiversity, and basic living spaces. Successful arrangements frame the models for making and overseeing such regions, taking into account natural importance and likely dangers.

Financial Motivations and Disincentives:

Integrating monetary instruments, like duties, endowments, and installments for environment administrations, empowers reasonable land use rehearses. Strategies can boost landowners to take part in preservation exercises or embrace eco-accommodating cultivating techniques, encouraging a harmony between financial interests and natural stewardship.

Administrative Measures:

Strong strategies incorporate administrative measures to uphold economical land use rehearses. This might include setting principles for contamination control, deforestation limits, and reasonable farming practices. Administrative structures guarantee consistence and stop exercises that present dangers to protection endeavors.

Challenges in Creating Viable Strategy Structures:

Political and Monetary Tensions:

Policymakers frequently face tensions to focus on momentary financial increases over long haul ecological supportability. Political contemplations and the impact of monetary interests can block the turn of events and execution of tough preservation arrangements.

Absence of Coordinated Approaches:

Divided strategies across various areas, like farming, ranger service, and metropolitan turn of events, can block powerful land use arranging. Coordinated approaches that consider the interconnectedness of environments and human exercises are fundamental for exhaustive arrangement structures.

Insufficient Authorization and Observing:

Feeble authorization components and lacking observing frameworks sabotage the adequacy of protection strategies. Without appropriate oversight and punishments for rebelliousness, approaches might come up short on teeth expected to forestall criminal operations and territory obliteration.

Social and Social Contemplations:

Disregarding friendly and social viewpoints in approach advancement can prompt opposition and rebelliousness. Perceiving the freedoms and necessities of nearby networks, native gatherings, and conventional land clients is vital for the outcome of strategies pointed toward adjusting preservation and human turn of events.

Examples of overcoming adversity:

Costa Rica's Installment for Environment Administrations (PES) Program:

Costa Rica's PES program remains as a worldwide example of overcoming adversity. The program remunerates landowners for saving backwoods and giving biological system administrations. By putting monetary worth on natural preservation, the strategy has prompted huge reforestation endeavors and the insurance of basic environments.

Germany's Coordinated Protection Strategies:

Germany's coordinated protection strategies grandstand the viability of an all encompassing methodology. The nation has carried out arrangements that interweave biodiversity protection with reasonable land use arranging, advancing green framework, and guaranteeing the availability of environments.

Possible Roads for Development:

Reinforcing Worldwide Joint effort:

Worldwide difficulties require worldwide arrangements. Improving worldwide joint effort ashore use and protection strategies can work with the sharing of best practices, innovation move, and the improvement of normalized systems that rise above public lines.

Incorporating Native Information:

Recognizing and integrating native information and customary land the board rehearses is significant. Native people group frequently have significant bits of knowledge into feasible land use and preservation, and their contribution in strategy improvement upgrades the odds of coming out on top.

Versatile Administration Approaches:

Embracing versatile administration approaches recognizes the powerful idea of biological systems and human social orders. Strategies ought to be adaptable, taking into account changes in view of new data, evolving conditions, and criticism from partners.

Putting resources into Innovation and Information Examination:

Saddling innovation, including satellite symbolism, remote detecting, and information investigation, upgrades the observing and implementation abilities of preservation strategies. Ongoing information can give experiences into land cover changes, deforestation, and biological system wellbeing.

6.1 National and International Conservation Policies

Preservation approaches, both at the public and worldwide levels, are basic instruments in tending to the worldwide test of biodiversity misfortune and ecological debasement. While public strategies shape the administration of normal assets inside borders, global cooperation becomes vital for tending to transboundary natural issues. This investigation digs into the intricacies of public and worldwide protection strategies, inspecting their key parts, difficulties, triumphs, and the cooperative pathways required for a manageable future.

Public Protection Strategies:

Safeguarded Regions and Biodiversity Protection:

Public preservation strategies frequently base on the foundation and the executives of safeguarded regions. These regions, assigned to monitor biodiversity and biological systems, act as the foundation of public protection endeavors. Arrangements frame the rules for the creation and the board of these areas, offsetting biological importance with the necessities of neighborhood networks.

Reasonable Asset The executives:

Strategies advancing reasonable asset the executives plan to manage exercises like logging, fishing, and horticulture to guarantee that normal assets are used in a manner that keeps up with natural equilibrium. This incorporates setting quantities, managing extraction strategies, and carrying out measures to forestall overexploitation.

Financial Motivators for Protection:

Numerous public approaches consolidate monetary instruments to boost preservation endeavors. These may incorporate assessment motivators for eco-accommodating practices, endowments for maintainable horticulture, and installments for biological system administrations. By connecting financial worth to preservation, strategies energize a harmony between monetary turn of events and natural stewardship.

Natural Effect Appraisals (EIAs):

Public preservation approaches frequently require thorough EIAs for advancement projects. These appraisals assess the expected ecological effects of undertakings before they are supported, assisting with recognizing and alleviate likely mischief to biological systems, biodiversity, and regular assets.

Challenges in Public Preservation Approaches:

Clashing Interests:

Offsetting preservation objectives with financial interests can challenge. Contending requests for land, assets, and improvement frequently lead to clashes between protection strategies and areas focusing on financial development.

Implementation and Consistence:

Frail requirement instruments and lacking checking can subvert the viability of public preservation arrangements. Stricter implementation, supported by punishments for resistance, is fundamental to guarantee that strategies are carried out on the ground.

Restricted Assets:

Numerous countries face asset limitations, restricting their ability to execute and implement vigorous preservation arrangements. Sufficient subsidizing, limit building, and specialized help are fundamental for making an interpretation of approaches into substantial preservation results.

Native Privileges and Neighborhood People group:

Public arrangements should explore the sensitive harmony between preservation objectives and the privileges of native people groups and neighborhood networks. Inability to think about their privileges and include them in dynamic cycles can prompt opposition and incapability of preservation strategies.

Examples of overcoming adversity in Public Protection Approaches:

Costa Rica's Spearheading Protection Model:

Costa Rica is praised for its dynamic protection approaches. The country's Installment for Biological system Administrations (PES) program monetarily rewards landowners for saving timberlands and giving environment administrations. This drive has prompted expanded woods cover, biodiversity protection, and local area commitment.

Namibia's People group Based Protection:

Namibia's protection arrangements focus on local area contribution in overseeing normal assets. By allowing neighborhood networks freedoms over natural life the board and the travel industry, Namibia has effectively incorporated protection with rustic turn of events, prompting expanded untamed life populaces and financial advantages for nearby occupants.

Worldwide Protection Arrangements:

Multilateral Natural Arrangements (MEAs):

Worldwide preservation is in many cases administered by MEAs, which are arrangements haggled between various countries. Shows like the Show on Natural Variety

(CBD), the Ramsar Show on Wetlands, and the Show on Worldwide Exchange Jeopardized Types of Wild Fauna and Verdure (Refers to) give structures to cooperative activity on worldwide ecological issues.

Worldwide Natural Administration:

Worldwide foundations, for example, the Unified Countries Climate Program (UNEP) and the Intergovernmental Board on Biodiversity and Biological system Administrations (IPBES), assume a significant part in organizing global endeavors for protection. These organizations work with information sharing, coordinate worldwide drives, and give a stage to countries to address ecological difficulties on the whole.

Transboundary Preservation Drives:

Given the interconnected idea of environments, numerous preservation strategies have a transboundary center. Global coordinated efforts on shared biological systems, for example, the Amazon Rainforest or the Incomparable Obstruction Reef, include composed endeavors to address normal difficulties and guarantee the feasible administration of shared assets.

Subsidizing Components:

Worldwide subsidizing instruments, including the Worldwide Climate Office (GEF) and the Green Environment Asset, support protection projects around the world. These assets plan to connect monetary holes, empowering non-industrial countries to carry out protection strategies and address ecological difficulties.

Challenges in Worldwide Protection Strategies:

Restricted Implementation Systems:

Worldwide protection arrangements frequently need strong authorization components. While MEAs set out wide standards, the capacity to urge countries to agree is restricted, and authorizes for rebelliousness are frequently feeble.

Sway and Public Interests:

Offsetting worldwide protection objectives with public power and interests can challenge. Countries might focus on their financial improvement over worldwide protection commitments, prompting pressures and clashes in executing shared strategies.

Unjust Appropriation of Advantages:

Worldwide preservation endeavors should resolve issues of value. There is much of the time an irregularity in the dispersion of advantages, with non-industrial countries bearing the weight of preservation yet not receiving similar benefits. Guaranteeing decency in worldwide protection drives is significant for long haul achievement.

Examples of overcoming adversity in Global Preservation Arrangements:

Antarctic Deal Framework:

The Antarctic Settlement Framework, endorsed by different countries, assigns Antarctica as a logical save and boycotts military action on the landmass. This global cooperation has effectively shielded a novel and perfect climate from expected double-dealing.

UNESCO World Legacy Locales:

The UNESCO World Legacy Destinations program assigns and safeguards social and regular locales of extraordinary all inclusive worth. This worldwide drive has added to the safeguarding of famous normal milestones, like the Galápagos Islands and Yellowstone Public Park.

Expected Roads for Development:

Reinforcing Consistence Systems:

Improving worldwide protection approaches requires more grounded consistence instruments. This might include making additional authoritative arrangements, expanding straightforwardness, and laying out ramifications for countries that neglect to meet their responsibilities.

Coordinating Neighborhood Information and Inclusion:

Perceiving the significance of neighborhood information and including nearby networks in global preservation drives is pivotal. Consolidating different points of view guarantees that strategies are socially delicate and bound to prevail on the ground.

Tending to Environmental Change:

Global preservation approaches need to incorporate endeavors to address environmental change. Environmental change intensifies existing natural difficulties and requires a planned worldwide reaction to relieve its effects on biological systems and biodiversity.

Advancing Practical Improvement Objectives (SDGs):

Adjusting protection strategies to more extensive practical improvement objectives, like those framed in the Unified Countries Manageable Advancement Objectives (SDGs), cultivates a comprehensive methodology. Coordination with objectives connected with neediness lightening, wellbeing, and instruction upgrades the viability of protection endeavors.

6.2 Zoning and Land Use Regulations

Drafting and land use guidelines are primary parts of metropolitan preparation and administration, employing huge impact over the physical, social, and financial scene of networks. These guidelines are fundamental apparatuses in overseeing and adjusting the contending interests of improvement, protection, and local area prosperity. This investigation dives into the multi-layered universe of drafting and land use guidelines, analyzing their verifiable advancement, key standards, contemporary difficulties, and the crucial job they play in cultivating feasible turn of events.

Verifiable Advancement of Drafting:

The idea of drafting arose because of the quick urbanization and industrialization of the late nineteenth and mid twentieth hundreds of years. As urban communities extended, worries about general wellbeing, security, and the need to isolate incongruent land utilizes prompted the advancement of drafting laws. Outstanding achievements in the verifiable development of drafting include:

Euclidean Drafting (1920s):

The Euclidean drafting model, named after the U.S. High Legal dispute Town of Euclid v. Ambler Realty Co., presented separating land into unmistakable zones in view of purpose. Private, business, and modern purposes were isolated to alleviate possible contentions and improve public government assistance.

Drafting for Complete Preparation (1930s-1950s):

The mid-twentieth century saw a shift towards complete preparation, with drafting developing to think about more extensive local area objectives. Drafting laws started to consolidate components of land use arranging, natural contemplations, and local area feel.

Adaptable Drafting (1960s-1970s):

The 1960s and 1970s saw a move towards more adaptable drafting guidelines. Arranging specialists began exploring different avenues regarding blended use drafting, overlay locale, and execution based drafting, taking into account more prominent flexibility to developing local area needs.

Brilliant Development and Manageable Drafting (1980s-Present):

In late many years, there has been a developing accentuation on manageable turn of events and savvy development standards in drafting. Networks are progressively taking on guidelines that focus on ecological protection, walkability, and the effective utilization of assets.

Key Standards of Drafting and Land Use Guidelines:

Land Use Classifications:

Drafting guidelines regularly partition land into classifications in view of purpose, for example, private, business, modern, and sporting. This isolation forestalls incongruent land utilizes from existing together and advances precise turn of events.

Thickness and Power Controls:

Drafting guidelines frequently incorporate arrangements for controlling the thickness and power of advancement. This includes determining the greatest number of abiding units per section of land, building level cutoff points, and floor region proportions to deal with the general size of improvement.

Difficulty and Building Arrangement:

Misfortune prerequisites direct the distance between a construction and the property line. These guidelines mean to guarantee sufficient dividing between structures, keep up with protection, and add to a strong streetscape.

Drafting Overlay Areas:

Overlay locale are extra drafting guidelines that might be applied to explicit regions inside a local area. They address interesting contemplations, like memorable conservation, ecological assurance, or plan principles, past the fundamental land use classes.

Blended Use Drafting:

Perceiving the advantages of blended use improvement, some drafting mandates grant a mix of private, business, and sporting purposes inside a solitary region. This approach cultivates walkable networks, lessens dependence on autos, and advances social cooperation.

Contemporary Difficulties in Drafting and Land Use Guidelines:

Moderateness and Lodging:

Drafting guidelines can add to lodging moderateness challenges by restricting the thickness of improvement. Exclusionary drafting rehearses, for example, least part sizes and limitations on multifamily lodging, can worsen lodging deficiencies and reasonableness issues.

Value and Civil rights:

Drafting has generally been connected to social imbalances, frequently isolating networks in view of financial elements. Contemporary difficulties incorporate tending to past shameful acts and guaranteeing that drafting advances comprehensive turn of events, giving fair admittance to assets and potential open doors.

Environmental Change and Strength:

Drafting and land use guidelines should adjust to the difficulties presented by environmental change. This incorporates contemplations for ocean level ascent, outrageous climate occasions, and the mix of green foundation to improve local area versatility.

Innovation and Metropolitan Advancement:

Quick mechanical headways and the ascent of savvy urban communities present provokes in adjusting drafting guidelines to oblige advancements like independent vehicles, drone conveyance administrations, and computerized foundation. Drafting codes should be adequately adaptable to embrace innovative headways while tending to related gambles.

Examples of overcoming adversity in Drafting and Feasible Turn of events:

Portland, Oregon - Metropolitan Development Limit:

Portland's way to deal with metropolitan arranging incorporates the foundation of a Metropolitan Development Limit (UGB) to contain endless suburbia. This limit empowers conservative advancement inside as far as possible, advancing walkability and safeguarding provincial scenes.

Vancouver, Canada - Laneway Lodging:

Vancouver has effectively tended to lodging difficulties by executing drafting strategies that consider the development of laneway houses in existing neighborhoods. This imaginative methodology increments lodging choices without altogether modifying the personality of neighborhoods.

Likely Roads for Development:

Straightforwardness and Local area Commitment:

Upgrading straightforwardness in the drafting system and it are basic to advance local area commitment. Giving open data and including occupants in direction guarantees that drafting guidelines line up with local area values and needs.

Versatile Drafting:

Drafting codes ought to embrace flexibility to oblige developing local area needs and mechanical headways. Taking on execution based drafting, structure based codes, and consistently refreshing guidelines can add to a more responsive and dynamic arranging system.

Value Focused Drafting:

Drafting guidelines ought to effectively address social value concerns. This includes reconsidering drafting rehearses that sustain isolation, advancing reasonable lodging, and guaranteeing that networks have fair admittance to conveniences and administrations.

Integrating Green and Maintainable Plan:

Coordinating economical plan standards into drafting guidelines advances harmless to the ecosystem improvement. This might incorporate boosting green structure works on, requiring energy-effective plans, and integrating green spaces into metropolitan preparation.

6.3 Challenges and Opportunities in Policy Implementation

Strategy definition is just the most vital phase in the mind boggling venture towards cultural change. The viability of any strategy relies on effective execution, an interaction full of difficulties yet ready with open doors. This investigation dives into the complex domain of strategy execution, looking at the obstacles policymakers face, the potential open doors for development and improvement, and the unique exchange among approaches and this present reality settings where they unfurl.

Challenges in Arrangement Execution:

Protection from Change:

One of the lasting provokes in arrangement execution is protection from change. People and associations might be impervious to modifying laid out rehearses, in any event, when faced with the need of strategy driven change. Conquering this inactivity requires successful correspondence, commitment, and an unmistakable comprehension of the advantages of the proposed changes.

Absence of Assets:

Lacking assets, both monetary and human, can block strategy execution. Arrangements frequently request financing, gifted faculty, and mechanical framework. At the point when these assets are inadequate with regards to, it can prompt deferrals, compromised quality, or even the altogether disappointment of execution endeavors.

Complex Interdependencies:

Strategies only from time to time exist in seclusion; they are essential for a trap of interconnected frameworks and cycles. Understanding and exploring the mind boggling interdependencies between different areas, partners, and strategies represents a test. Potentially negative results and clashes might emerge, requesting a nuanced way to deal with strategy execution.

Deficient Correspondence:

Powerful correspondence is principal for fruitful arrangement execution. Ineffectively conveyed strategies can prompt disarray, falsehood, and opposition. Policymakers should put resources into clear, straightforward, and comprehensive correspondence techniques to guarantee that partners figure out the targets, reasoning, and anticipated results of the approach.

Absence of Checking and Assessment:

Carrying out arrangements without hearty observing and assessment instruments can obstruct the capacity to survey their effect. Routinely following headway, assessing results, and making information driven changes are fundamental for viable approach execution. The shortfall of these cycles might bring about an absence of responsibility and the propagation of insufficient strategies.

Amazing open doors in Arrangement Execution:

Creative Innovations:

The advanced age has introduced uncommon open doors for strategy execution. Developments, for example, information examination, man-made consciousness, and blockchain offer instruments for upgraded checking, smoothed out processes, and further developed direction. Policymakers can use innovation to make execution more proficient and responsive.

Local area Commitment and Investment:

Local area commitment is a strong chance for effective strategy execution. Including people group in the dynamic cycle, looking for their feedback, and consolidating neighborhood information can improve the significance and acknowledgment of approaches. Drawn in networks are bound to help and effectively add to the progress of carried out approaches.

Public-Private Organizations (PPPs):

Joint effort between general society and confidential areas presents open doors for asset sharing and advancement. Public-private associations (PPPs) can bring different mastery, financing, and productivity to strategy execution endeavors. These joint efforts are especially pertinent in regions where the public authority might miss the mark on assets or mastery to freely carry out strategies.

Limit Building and Preparing:

Putting resources into limit building and preparing programs is a valuable chance to beat the test of deficient HR. Outfitting staff with the essential abilities and information upgrades their capacity to really carry out approaches. Persistent preparation guarantees that the labor force stays versatile to developing strategy prerequisites.

Versatile Administration Approaches:

Embracing versatile administration approaches recognizes the powerful idea of strategy execution. Adaptability and the capacity to gain for a fact empower policymakers to change procedures because of evolving conditions. This versatile attitude can transform difficulties into open doors for iterative improvement.

True Models:

Singapore's Shrewd Country Drive:

Singapore's Shrewd Country drive epitomizes the utilization of creative advances in strategy execution. The city-state use information investigation, the Web of Things (IoT), and advanced answers for improve metropolitan living, transportation, and public administrations. The joining of innovation permits policymakers to screen and answer metropolitan difficulties progressively.

Estonia's E-Government Change:

Estonia's obligation to e-administration delineates the capability of innovation in arrangement execution. Through a solid computerized framework, Estonia has smoothed out managerial cycles, from e-residency to computerized marks. This advanced change has further developed proficiency as well as upgraded resident commitment and fulfillment.

New York City's Vision Zero:

New York City's Vision Zero drive is a great representation of local area commitment in strategy execution. The program expects to take out traffic fatalities through a mix of framework upgrades, instruction, and requirement. By including networks and partners in the dynamic cycle, the city has seen a decrease in rush hour gridlock related fatalities.

Costa Rica's Installment for Environment Administrations (PES) Program:

Costa Rica's prosperity with the PES program shows the positive results of public-private organizations. By boosting landowners to ration backwoods and give environment administrations, Costa Rica has accomplished huge reforestation and biodiversity preservation.

The coordinated effort between the public authority, confidential area, and neighborhood networks has been urgent to the program's prosperity.

Procedures for Powerful Approach Execution:

Clear Correspondence and Partner Commitment:

Straightforward correspondence and dynamic partner commitment are central to effective approach execution. Clear enunciation of strategy objectives, advantages, and assumptions encourages understanding and backing. Drawing in partners early and during the cycle guarantees that different points of view are thought of.

Information Driven Independent direction:

Tackling the force of information for dynamic improves the accuracy and viability of strategy execution. Information examination and checking instruments empower policymakers to follow progress, distinguish bottlenecks, and make informed changes. Normal information driven assessments give experiences to nonstop improvement.

Adaptability and Flexibility:

Arrangements ought to be planned in view of adaptability. Recognizing that unanticipated difficulties might emerge considers versatile reactions. Persistent checking, input circles, and a readiness to change methodologies in light of proof add to the nimbleness expected for fruitful execution.

Limit Building and Preparing Projects:

Fortifying the limit of people and associations engaged with execution is pivotal. Putting resources into preparing programs, expertise improvement, and information move guarantees that the labor force is prepared to actually execute arrangements. Consistent learning encourages a culture of development and improvement.

Coordinated effort and Organizations:

Cooperation, both inside government offices and through organizations with the confidential area and common society, upgrades the aggregate limit with regards to strategy execution. Shared assets, skill, and obligations add to a more extensive and powerful methodology.

Chapter 7

Community Engagement In Land Use Conservation

Land use protection is a complex undertaking that requires dynamic contribution and cooperation from the networks straightforwardly impacted by these endeavors. Local area commitment in land use protection isn't simply a checkbox in the policy-making system; a basic part shapes the achievement and supportability of preservation drives. This investigation digs into the significance of local area commitment in land use preservation, the different structures it can take, and the extraordinary effect it can have on the two environments and the prosperity of nearby occupants.

The Meaning of Local area Commitment in Land Use Preservation:

Nearby Information and Skill:

Networks frequently have significant neighborhood information about the environments they occupy. This information, went down through ages, incorporates bits of knowledge into the way of behaving of neighborhood widely varied vegetation, the occasional examples of natural life, and conventional land the executives rehearses. Drawing in with neighborhood networks takes advantage of this abundance of data, enhancing preservation endeavors with a nuanced comprehension of the nearby climate.

Social Association with the Land:

Numerous people group share a profound social and otherworldly association with their territory. For native people groups and nearby networks, the scene isn't simply an actual space yet a vault of social legacy and personality. Perceiving and regarding this association is fundamental for cultivating a feeling of responsibility and stewardship that goes past administrative measures.

Shared Liability and Stewardship:

Compelling area use preservation requires a common feeling of obligation for the climate. By including networks in dynamic cycles, preservation drives become co-operative undertakings as opposed to burdens. This common obligation cultivates a feeling of stewardship, where networks effectively partake in the security and economical administration of their normal assets.

Improved Viability of Strategies:

Arrangements planned without the info and purchase in of neighborhood networks might confront opposition or unseen side-effects. Drawing in networks in the arrangement plan process guarantees that guidelines are logically pertinent, line up with local area needs, and are bound to be complied to. This improves the general adequacy of land use preservation arrangements.

Social and Financial Advantages:

Drawing in networks in land use protection can yield social and financial advantages. Preservation drives that consider the prosperity of neighborhood inhabitants might prompt the advancement of practical livelihoods, ecotourism potential open doors, and further developed admittance to biological system administrations. This, thusly, fortifies the association between protection objectives and the more extensive interests of the local area.

Types of Local area Commitment in Land Use Protection:

Participatory Direction:

Effectively including local area individuals in dynamic cycles enables them to contribute their points of view, concerns, and goals. This can appear as local gatherings, studios, or participatory arranging meetings where local area individuals have an immediate say in forming preservation techniques.

Cooperative Exploration and Checking:

Connecting with networks in exploration and observing exercises changes them into dynamic accomplices in the protection cycle. This cooperative methodology creates significant information as well as constructs nearby limit and cultivates a feeling of pride over the results. Networks become stewards of their own biological systems.

Training and Limit Building:

Training is an incredible asset for local area commitment. Giving data about the significance of land use preservation, the natural meaning of specific regions, and the possible effects of human exercises helps bring issues to light. Limit building drives, like preparation programs, engage local area individuals to take part in protection endeavors effectively.

Social Trade and Combination:

Understanding and regarding the social acts of neighborhood networks is fundamental for fruitful commitment. Social trade programs, where protectionists and local area individuals share bits of knowledge and gain from one another, can connect holes in understanding and encourage cooperative connections based on common regard.

Comprehensive Arrangements and Legitimate Structures:

Making strategies and lawful systems that effectively incorporate the points of view and freedoms of neighborhood networks is a type of commitment in itself. This includes perceiving and regarding native land privileges, guaranteeing impartial admittance to assets, and integrating conventional environmental information into administrative systems.

Genuine Instances of Effective People group Commitment:

Namibian People group Based Protection:

Namibia's people group based protection model is a demonstration of the force of connecting with neighborhood networks. By conceding collective conservancy privileges to neighborhood inhabitants, Namibia has effectively incorporated preservation with provincial turn of events. Networks are effectively engaged with untamed life the executives, benefit from the travel industry incomes, and assume a vital part in fighting poaching.

Costa Rica's Installment for Biological system Administrations (PES) Program:

Costa Rica's PES program draws in landowners in protection by monetarily compensating them for saving woodlands and giving environment administrations. This market-based approach esteems the ecological commitments of landowners, making an immediate motivation for preservation while helping nearby networks monetarily.

Maasai Mara Conservancies, Kenya:

In the Maasai Mara area of Kenya, people group claimed conservancies have been laid out to include nearby networks in untamed life protection. These conservancies permit Maasai people group to profit from untamed life the travel industry while effectively taking part in preservation endeavors. The methodology has diminished human-untamed life struggle and added to the conservation of basic environments.

Challenges in Local area Commitment:

Dissimilar Interests and Needs:

Networks are assorted, and individual interests and needs might vary. Adjusting the assorted requirements of local area individuals while chasing after all-encompassing protection objectives can challenge. Open correspondence and comprehensive dynamic cycles are fundamental to explore these distinctions.

Verifiable Question:

Verifiable question between protection associations and nearby networks can represent a critical hindrance to powerful commitment. This doubt might originate from previous encounters of abuse, underestimation, or the burden of protection measures without local area inclusion. Remaking trust requires a promise to straightforward, cooperative methodologies.

Limit and Information Holes:

A few networks might confront limit and information holes that block their dynamic support in preservation endeavors. This can incorporate restricted admittance to training, data, and assets. Tending to these holes requires designated limit building drives and instructive projects custom-made to the particular necessities of every local area.

Power Elements and Portrayal:

Power elements inside networks and among networks and outer preservation entertainers can influence the adequacy of commitment. Guaranteeing fair portrayal and keeping away from the convergence of dynamic power in a couple of people or gatherings is critical. Enabling minimized voices is fundamental for impartial commitment.

Outer Tensions and Worldwide Impacts:

Worldwide monetary powers and outer tensions can impact neighborhood networks and their relationship with their current circumstance. Financial impetuses, global market requests, and international variables might apply aberrant effect on nearby navigation. Moderating these tensions requires a nuanced comprehension of worldwide nearby elements.

Techniques for Powerful People group Commitment:

Comprehensive and Straightforward Correspondence:

Clear and comprehensive correspondence is fundamental for powerful commitment. Giving data in open configurations, utilizing neighborhood dialects, and utilizing different correspondence directs guarantee that everybody locally can partake in the discourse. Straightforward correspondence fabricates trust and works with informed direction.

Building Organizations with Neighborhood Pioneers:

Laying out organizations with neighborhood pioneers and powerhouses can improve the adequacy of local area commitment. Believed people group figures can act as extensions between preservation associations and occupants, working with exchange, and exploring social subtleties.

Fitting Ways to deal with Social Settings:

Perceiving and regarding social settings is fundamental for fruitful commitment. Ways to deal with commitment ought to be adaptable and adjusted to the particular social standards, customs, and upsides of every local area. Social responsiveness cultivates a more significant and conscious joint effort.

Enabling Ladies and Underestimated Gatherings:

Effectively including ladies and underestimated bunches in dynamic cycles is significant for comprehensive commitment. Enabling these voices guarantees a variety of points of view and helps address verifiable lopsided characteristics in power and portrayal.

Monetary Motivations and Business Backing:

Connecting preservation endeavors with financial impetuses for nearby networks is a strong commitment methodology. Giving elective job open doors, supporting feasible agribusiness, and making roads for money age can adjust protection objectives to the monetary prosperity of local area individuals.

7.1 Involving Local Communities in Decision-Making

In the domain of administration, perceiving the organization and skill of neighborhood networks isn't simply a question of procedural convention; it is a foundation of successful and practical direction. The contribution of neighborhood networks in the dynamic cycle is a vote based rule that guarantees strategies and drives line up with the requirements, yearnings, and relevant real factors of individuals they straightforwardly influence. This investigation digs into the meaning of including neighborhood networks in navigation, the different structures this cooperation can take, the difficulties in question, and the groundbreaking potential it holds for making strong and comprehensive social orders.

The Meaning of Including Neighborhood People group in Direction:

Logical Comprehension and Nearby Information:

Nearby people group have a personal comprehension of their environmental elements, molded by ages of lived encounters. This neighborhood information is a significant asset that policymakers can take advantage of while pursuing choices that influence the climate, land use, and local area prosperity. Including people group guarantees that choices are grounded in the nuanced comprehension of nearby settings.

Possession and Responsibility:

Including people group in dynamic cultivates a feeling of responsibility and responsibility. At the point when people effectively partake in forming strategies and drives, they are bound to feel an individual stake in their prosperity.

This feeling of pride converts into an aggregate liability regarding the results, empowering more noteworthy consistence and responsibility.

Social Pertinence and Responsiveness:

Nearby people group frequently have unmistakable social practices, customs, and values that impact their lifestyle. Including them in navigation guarantees that arrangements regard and line up with these social subtleties. This social awareness is fundamental for encouraging agreeable connections between administration structures and various local area characters.

Responsive and Versatile Arrangements:

Nearby people group are many times the first to encounter the effects of natural changes, financial movements, or social difficulties. Their immediate experience positions them as forefront spectators, fit for giving continuous bits of knowledge. Including people group in direction empowers the detailing of responsive and versatile arrangements that address arising issues expeditiously.

Social Union and Inclusivity:

Dynamic that incorporates assorted voices from neighborhood networks advances social union and inclusivity. It separates hindrances, lessens imbalances, and makes a more delegate and just administration structure. Inclusivity in navigation isn't just about variety for portrayal; it is tied in with recognizing and esteeming the extravagance of viewpoints that different networks offer that might be of some value.

Types of Including Nearby People group in Direction:

Participatory Preparation and Studios:

Coordinating participatory arranging meetings and studios permits local area individuals to effectively contribute thoughts, experiences, and concerns. These meetings can be organized to resolve explicit issues like metropolitan turn of events, natural preservation, or local area foundation. Participating in cooperative arranging encourages a feeling of co-creation.

Local area Meetings and Input Instruments:

Laying out conventional channels for local area conferences and criticism instruments guarantees that leaders get input straightforwardly from those impacted by arrangements. This can appear as formal reviews, overviews, or standard official Q&A events where local area individuals can offer their viewpoints and raise concerns.

Cooperative Exploration and Information Assortment:

Drawing in neighborhood networks in examination and information assortment exercises enables them with the apparatuses to contribute considerably to direction. This cooperative methodology creates important information as well as fabricates nearby limit and guarantees that the data gathered is logically pertinent.

Nearby Portrayal in Dynamic Bodies:

Effectively remembering neighborhood delegates for dynamic bodies, chambers, or warning gatherings guarantees that local area viewpoints are straightforwardly incorporated into the dynamic interaction. This portrayal can be formal, with assigned seats for local area pioneers, or casual, with standard conferences with local area agents.

Advanced Stages for Cooperation:

Utilizing advanced stages and innovation considers more extensive and more comprehensive interest. Online discussions, web-based entertainment, and portable applications can be utilized to accumulate input, share data, and work with conversations. This approach is especially applicable for connecting with different networks and those in remote or blocked off regions.

True Instances of Effective People group Contribution:

Bhutan's Gross Public Satisfaction (GNH) File:

Bhutan's remarkable way to deal with administration includes estimating the country's prosperity in monetary terms as well as concerning Gross Public Joy (GNH). The GNH Record integrates inputs from nearby networks through reviews and conferences, guaranteeing that approaches line up with the prosperity and upsides of individuals.

Participatory Planning in Porto Alegre, Brazil:

Porto Alegre in Brazil spearheaded the idea of participatory planning, where residents effectively participate in the distribution of metropolitan assets. Through a progression of local area congregations and conversations, occupants add to concluding how public assets are disseminated, considering direct local area input in monetary choices.

Local area Based Backwoods The executives in Nepal:

Nepal's People group Ranger service Program includes nearby networks in the administration and protection of woods. Networks are conceded freedoms to oversee assigned backwoods regions, and independent direction includes popularity based processes inside the local area. This approach has added to worked on woods protection and maintainable asset the executives.

Challenges in Including Neighborhood People group in Direction:

Power Irregular characteristics and Underestimation:

Existing power irregular characteristics and underestimation can thwart significant local area inclusion. Now and again, certain gatherings inside networks might be avoided from dynamic cycles, propagating disparities. Addressing power elements requires conscious endeavors to incorporate minimized voices.

Restricted Assets and Limit:

Nearby people group might confront constraints with regards to assets, information, and ability to effectively take part in direction. This challenge is especially articulated in monetarily hindered or distant regions. Connecting these holes requires designated limit building drives and asset allotment.

Protection from Change and Conventional Practices:

Protection from change, frequently established in conventional practices, can hinder local area association. A few networks might be reluctant to embrace new administration designs or innovations. Defeating this challenge includes building trust, regarding customs, and actually imparting the advantages of proposed changes.

Hypocrisy and Shallow Commitment:

Shallow types of commitment, for example, tokenistic conferences without certified thought of local area input, can prompt disappointment and doubt. It is vital for move past performative signals and guarantee that local area inclusion is meaningful, effective, and necessary to dynamic cycles.

Correspondence Hindrances and Language Variety:

Correspondence obstructions, including language variety, can upset successful commitment. In multicultural settings, guaranteeing that data is open in different dialects and that correspondence channels are comprehensive is significant. Defeating language hindrances cultivates a more comprehensive dynamic climate.

Systems for Successful People group Contribution:

Develop Trust Through Straightforward Correspondence:

Building trust is central for successful local area contribution. Straightforward and clear correspondence about the dynamic cycle, the targets of arrangements, and the normal results develops trust. Giving data in open configurations and dialects is fundamental for comprehensive correspondence.

Advance Comprehensive Portrayal:

Effectively advance comprehensive portrayal by guaranteeing that dynamic bodies incorporate different voices. This incorporates orientation variety, portrayal of various age gatherings, and consideration of minimized networks. Making roads for impartial portrayal guarantees that an expansive range of points of view is thought of.

Put resources into Local area Limit Building:

Put resources into building the limit of nearby networks to effectively partake in direction. This includes giving schooling, preparing, and assets to upgrade local area's comprehension individuals might interpret administration processes, empowering them to genuinely contribute.

Work with Exchange and Open Gatherings:

Make spaces for open exchange and gatherings where local area individuals can offer their viewpoints, get clarification on some pressing issues, and take part in useful conversations. These discussions can appear as municipal events, local area gatherings, or online stages, encouraging a culture of open correspondence.

Take on Adaptable and Comprehensive Methodologies:

Perceive and regard the variety of networks by taking on adaptable and comprehensive methodologies. This incorporates fitting commitment methodologies to social settings, obliging different correspondence styles, and guaranteeing that dynamic cycles are versatile to neighborhood needs.

7.2 Indigenous Perspectives on Land Use

Native people group all over the planet convey an abundance of information and a significant association with the land that traverses ages. Their viewpoints ashore use are well established in a comprehensive comprehension of the climate, stressing concordance, maintainability, and the reliance of every living thing. This investigation digs into the Native viewpoints ashore use, featuring the significant insight implanted in their customary practices and the examples they offer for contemporary ways to deal with protection and asset the executives.

Comprehensive Relationship with the Land:

Native viewpoints ashore use are described by an all encompassing relationship with the climate. Instead of review the land as a ware, Native people group see it as a living element with which they share an equal relationship. This comprehensive comprehension stretches out past the actual parts of the land to envelop otherworldly, social, and social aspects. The land isn't just an asset; it is a wellspring of personality, food, and otherworldliness.

Feasible Asset The board:

Key to Native land use points of view is the idea of economical asset the board. Conventional practices include a profound information on environments, occasional cycles, and biodiversity. Native people group have generally utilized maintainable reaping procedures, like rotational horticulture and specific gathering, to guarantee that assets are utilized in a manner that considers regular recovery and congruity.

Social Importance and Otherworldly Association:

Land holds significant social and otherworldly importance for Native people group. It isn't only a setting for human exercises yet a consecrated space interlaced with social practices, functions, and narrating. The otherworldly association with the land is many times communicated through customs that recognize the proportional connection among people and the regular world. Saving the land isn't just a natural basic yet a social and profound obligation.

Elderly folks as Attendants of Insight:

In Native people group, seniors assume an essential part as the guardians of shrewdness in regards to land use. Through oral customs, narrating, and lived encounters, older folks pass down information about reasonable practices, the meaning of explicit scenes, and the intergenerational obligations attached to really focusing on the land. The insight of elderly folks fills in as a directing power in dynamic inside Native people group.

Social Scenes and Conventional Domains:

Native viewpoints ashore use are personally attached to the idea of conventional regions. These are geological spaces as well as include a complicated trap of social scenes, tribal information, and local area chronicles. The acknowledgment of Native people groups' freedoms to their conventional regions is major to regarding their viewpoints ashore use and recognizing the effects of verifiable dispossession.

Difficulties to Native Land Use:

Regardless of the extravagance of Native viewpoints ashore use, these networks frequently face critical difficulties. Infringement on conventional regions, asset extraction, and natural debasement present dangers to both the land and the social practices established in it. Also, the inconvenience of outside preservation models that don't line up with Native qualities can prompt struggles and subvert the maintainability of conventional land use rehearses.

Contemporary Pertinence and Cooperative Preservation:

Native viewpoints ashore utilize offer significant experiences that are progressively perceived for their pertinence in tending to contemporary ecological difficulties. Cooperative protection moves toward that include Native people group as accomplices instead of subjects are getting some forward momentum. Such drives recognize the skill of Native people groups in economical asset the board and look to coordinate customary information with contemporary preservation procedures.

Worldwide Instances of Native Drove Protection:

Gunditjmara Social Scene, Australia:

The Gunditjmara nation in Australia have effectively coordinated customary land the executives rehearses with present day protection endeavors. The Budj Bim Social Scene, an UNESCO World Legacy site, is an illustration of Native drove protection. Gunditjmara hydroponics frameworks, going back more than 6,600 years, have been perceived as complex instances of maintainable land use.

Haida Gwaii, Canada:

The Haida Country in Canada's Haida Gwaii archipelago has been at the very front of Native drove protection. Through the foundation of safeguarded regions and the execution of customary asset the executives rehearses, the Haida public are effectively engaged with protecting their social and natural legacy.

Maya Biosphere Hold, Guatemala:

In the Maya Biosphere Hold in Guatemala, Native Q'eqchi' and Poqomchi' people group assume a urgent part in manageable ranger service and biodiversity protection. Their conventional practices, like local area ranger service and agroforestry, add to the conservation of the district's remarkable environments.

7.3 Community-Based Conservation Initiatives

Local area based protection drives address a change in perspective in natural stewardship, perceiving that manageable preservation endeavors are best when established in the networks straightforwardly associated with the land. These drives engage neighborhood occupants to become dynamic members in the security and the board of their regular assets. This investigation digs into the standards, triumphs, challenges, and extraordinary capability of local area based preservation drives, displaying how cooperative endeavors at the grassroots level can drive significant and enduring change.

Standards of Local area Based Protection:

Neighborhood Strengthening:

At the core of local area based protection is the guideline of nearby strengthening. Rather than forcing hierarchical arrangements, these drives include networks in dynamic cycles, guaranteeing that occupants have something to do with the administration of their normal assets. This strengthening encourages a feeling of pride and obligation regarding the climate.

Social Significance:

Local area based protection perceives and regards the social setting of nearby networks. Customary information, rehearses, and social qualities are incorporated into preservation systems. This approach guarantees the protection of social legacy as well as improves the adequacy of preservation endeavors by adjusting them to the local area's lifestyle.

Cooperative Administration:

Joint effort is a foundation of local area based preservation. Neighborhood people group work in association with government offices, non-administrative associations (NGOs), and different partners. This cooperative administration model considers shared liability, asset sharing, and a variety of points of view in dynamic cycles.

Economical Occupations:

Perceiving the reliance among networks and their current circumstance, local area based protection means to upgrade supportable occupations. Preservation endeavors are intended to coincide with neighborhood monetary exercises, giving networks motivators for saving normal assets as opposed to taking advantage of them for transient additions.

Versatile Administration:

Local area based preservation embraces versatile administration standards. It recognizes that biological systems are dynamic and dependent upon future developments.

Thusly, drives are intended to be adaptable, considering changes in light of continuous checking, criticism from networks, and changing natural circumstances.

Examples of overcoming adversity of Local area Based Preservation Drives:

Nepal's People group Ranger service Program:

Nepal's People group Ranger service Program is an internationally acclaimed illustration of local area based preservation. Started in the last part of the 1970s, the program awards neighborhood networks the freedoms to reasonably oversee and use backwoods assets.

This approach has prompted expanded woods cover, further developed biodiversity, and upgraded local area versatility.

Namibian People group Based Regular Asset The board:

Namibia's People group Based Normal Asset The board (CBNRM) program enables nearby networks to oversee untamed life and regular assets. Through conservancies, networks participate in untamed life protection, the travel industry, and feasible asset use. The program has added to expanded untamed life populaces, financial advantages for networks, and reinforced protection associations.

Peru's Native Regional Stores:

Native Regional Stores (ITRs) in Peru represent local area based protection drove by native networks. These stores award native gatherings lawful privileges to their genealogical grounds, empowering them to safeguard both social legacy and biodiversity. The participatory administration of ITRs has demonstrated compelling in safeguarding timberlands and customary practices.

Challenges in Local area Based Protection:

Outside Tensions and Abuse:

Regardless of the standards of local area based protection, outer tensions, including financial interests and advancement projects, can undermine nearby environments. Networks might confront difficulties in opposing these tensions, particularly when confronted with financial motivating forces that appear to be more prompt than the drawn out advantages of protection.

Limit and Information Holes:

Networks took part in protection drives might experience limit and information holes. Restricted admittance to training and assets can block powerful cooperation. Crossing over these holes requires designated limit building endeavors, guaranteeing that networks have the right stuff and information required for supportable protection rehearses.

Social and Political Elements:

Social and political elements inside networks can impact the outcome of preservation drives. Unseen fits of turmoil, power lopsided characteristics, or conflicts about asset use can obstruct aggregate activity. It is fundamental for address these elements and encourage comprehensive dynamic cycles.

Deficient Approach Backing:

At times, local area based protection drives need sufficient strategy support. Lawful structures may not completely perceive the privileges and commitments of neighborhood networks. Adjusting approaches to the standards of local area based preservation is critical for establishing an empowering climate for grassroots drives.

Environmental Change and Outside Natural Variables:

Environmental change and outside ecological elements present difficulties to local area based preservation. Changing atmospheric conditions, catastrophic events, and outer natural stressors can influence the viability of preservation endeavors. Transformation techniques should be incorporated into local area based drives to address these difficulties.

Systems for Improving People group Based Protection:
Local area Commitment and Training:

Putting resources into local area commitment and training is central for effective local area based preservation. Building mindfulness about the significance of protection, giving preparation on manageable practices, and cultivating a feeling of natural stewardship engage networks to take part in preservation endeavors effectively.

Organizations and Cooperation:

Fortifying associations and coordinated effort between networks, legislative offices, NGOs, and different partners is fundamental. Cooperative endeavors influence different skill, assets, and backing, making a more exhaustive and viable way to deal with protection.

Motivating force Instruments:

Executing motivator instruments is vital for supporting local area based protection drives. This might incorporate monetary motivating forces, admittance to elective occupation open doors, or advantages from eco-the travel industry. Adjusting preservation objectives to local area prosperity makes a positive input circle for supported commitment.

Strategy Promotion and Legitimate Acknowledgment:

Pushing for strategy changes that perceive and uphold local area based protection is fundamental. Lawful acknowledgment of local area freedoms to regular assets and support in dynamic cycles fortifies the authenticity and effect of grassroots drives.

Versatile Administration and Checking:

Embracing versatile administration standards and carrying out vigorous checking frameworks consider constant learning and improvement. Ordinary evaluations of preservation results, local area interest, and the adequacy of procedures illuminate versatile reactions to evolving conditions.

Chapter 8

Technological Innovations in Monitoring Land Use Impact

Land use is a basic part of human progress, straightforwardly impacting the climate, economy, and society. As the worldwide populace keeps on developing, the interest for land builds, prompting changes in land use designs. Observing these progressions is fundamental for supportable turn of events, natural preservation, and viable land the board. Mechanical developments assume a vital part in upgrading our capacity to screen land use influence precisely and proficiently. This article investigates the different mechanical progressions that have altered the manner in which we screen land use influence, from satellite symbolism and remote detecting to cutting edge information examination and AI.

Satellite Symbolism and Remote Detecting

Quite possibly of the main mechanical leap forward in observing area use influence is the utilization of satellite symbolism and remote detecting. Satellites outfitted with high-goal cameras and sensors circle the Earth, catching itemized pictures of the planet's surface. This innovation gives a thorough and continuous perspective ashore use changes for a huge scope.

Satellite symbolism empowers the observing of deforestation, urbanization, horticultural development, and other land use changes with a degree of detail that was beforehand out of reach. Remote detecting advances, like LiDAR (Light Location and Going) and RADAR (Radio Identification and Running), improve our capacity to accumulate information in different weather patterns and geographic territories.

These innovations consider the recognizable proof of land cover types, the estimation of vegetation wellbeing, and the appraisal of land surface temperatures. For instance, satellites can recognize changes in woodland cover, screen horticultural practices, and distinguish regions inclined to ecological corruption.

AI and Computerized reasoning

The joining of AI (ML) and computerized reasoning (computer based intelligence) into land use observing has achieved exceptional headways in information examination and understanding. These innovations can deal with immense measures of satellite symbolism and remote detecting information, extricating significant bits of knowledge and patterns.

ML calculations can group land cover types, separate among normal and human-actuated changes, and foresee future land use designs. Artificial intelligence fueled frameworks can investigate authentic information to distinguish likely regions in danger of land corruption or evaluate the effect of explicit land use strategies. The blend of AI and satellite symbolism works with more exact and convenient dynamic in land the executives and protection endeavors.

Geographic Data Frameworks (GIS)

Geographic Data Frameworks (GIS) have become imperative apparatuses in observing and overseeing land use influence. GIS incorporates spatial information, like satellite symbolism, with non-spatial information, taking into account the making of point by point guides and models. This innovation empowers chiefs to imagine and dissect spatial examples, connections, and patterns connected with land use.

GIS applications help in land-use arranging, asset assignment, and natural effect evaluations. By overlaying various layers of data, GIS takes into account the distinguishing proof of regions powerless against explicit land use changes and supports the advancement of procedures to relieve adverse consequences. Furthermore, GIS works with coordinated effort and information dividing between various partners associated with land the executives.

Drones and Automated Airborne Vehicles (UAVs)

Drones and Automated Elevated Vehicles (UAVs) have arisen as integral assets for observing area use influence at an additional confined and nitty gritty level. These ethereal stages can catch high-goal symbolism, perform overviews, and gather information in regions that might be trying to get to or risky for human onlookers.

Drones outfitted with cutting edge sensors, for example, multispectral and hyper-spectral cameras, give important data about vegetation wellbeing, soil conditions, and land surface attributes. This information supports accuracy farming, environmental observing, and catastrophe reaction. UAVs are especially helpful in checking limited scope land use changes, like unlawful logging, mining exercises, and changes in land cover inside safeguarded regions.

Blockchain Innovation for Land The executives

Blockchain innovation, known for its part in secure and straightforward exchanges in the monetary area, is currently tracking down applications in land the board and checking. Blockchain offers a decentralized and carefully designed record framework that can be utilized to record and confirm land exchanges, possession, and land use changes.

By carrying out blockchain in land the board frameworks, it becomes conceivable to make a straightforward and permanent record of land exchanges.

This diminishes the gamble of deceitful exercises, guarantees secure land residency, and works on the most common way of confirming area proprietorship. Blockchain innovation can upgrade trust and straightforwardness in land use checking, particularly in locales where land residency is a petulant issue.

Web of Things (IoT) in Accuracy Horticulture

The Web of Things (IoT) has upset horticulture by giving constant information on different variables influencing crop wellbeing and efficiency. With regards to land use influence, IoT gadgets can be sent to screen soil conditions, weather conditions, and yield execution.

Sensors put in the field can gather information on soil dampness, supplement levels, and temperature. This data assists ranchers with settling on informed conclusions about water system, treatment, and nuisance control, eventually streamlining land use for maintainable rural practices. By coordinating IoT information with other observing innovations, a far reaching comprehension of the effect of rural exercises ashore can be accomplished.

Expanded Reality (AR) for Partner Commitment

Expanded Reality (AR) innovation upgrades partner commitment in land use observing by giving vivid and intelligent encounters. AR applications can overlay computerized data onto this present reality climate, permitting partners to imagine potential land use changes and their effects.

For instance, AR can be utilized to mimic the enhanced visualizations of a proposed foundation project on the encompassing scene. This empowers partners, including neighborhood networks and policymakers, to more readily comprehend the possible outcomes of explicit land use choices. AR adds to more educated and comprehensive dynamic cycles, cultivating coordinated effort and lessening clashes connected with land use changes.

Difficulties and Future Headings

While mechanical advancements have altogether worked on our capacity to screen land use influence, a few difficulties remain. The significant expense of trend setting innovations, information openness issues, and the requirement for talented experts to decipher complex informational indexes are among the hindrances that should be tended to.

Besides, the moral contemplations of involving innovation for land observing, including security concerns and the likely abuse of information, require cautious consideration. Finding some kind of harmony between mechanical progressions and moral contemplations is critical for the mindful and supportable utilization of these devices.

Looking forward, the fate of checking land use effect will probably include proceeded with headways in sensor innovation, AI calculations, and information examination. Mix of information from numerous sources and interdisciplinary joint effort will be fundamental for creating comprehensive ways to deal with land the board.

8.1 Remote Sensing and GIS Applications

Remote detecting and Geographic Data Frameworks (GIS) have become basic parts of present day mechanical headways, assuming an essential part in different fields, from ecological checking and normal asset the executives to metropolitan preparation and fiasco reaction. Remote detecting includes the assortment of data about the World's surface without direct actual contact, for the most part through satellite or flying stages, while GIS includes the investigation and translation of spatial information. This article investigates the far reaching utilizations of remote detecting and GIS, featuring their importance in various areas and their joined potential in giving significant experiences to leaders.

Natural Observing and Protection

One of the essential uses of remote detecting and GIS is in ecological observing and protection. Satellite symbolism gives a higher perspective of the Earth, permitting researchers and hippies to follow changes in land cover, deforestation, and biodiversity. Remote detecting helps in recognizing and checking environments, evaluating the wellbeing of vegetation, and concentrating on the effect of environmental change on normal territories.

GIS assumes a pivotal part in putting together and examining ecological information. It empowers the making of guides that show basic data, like the appropriation of imperiled species, safeguarded regions, and biodiversity areas of interest. By coordinating remote detecting and GIS, progressives can foster powerful procedures for living space protection, untamed life the executives, and the reclamation of biological systems.

Agribusiness and Accuracy Cultivating

Remote detecting and GIS have altered agribusiness by giving ranchers significant bits of knowledge for accuracy cultivating. Satellite symbolism and flying reviews can catch itemized data about crop wellbeing, soil conditions, and water system needs. This information assists ranchers with enhancing their agrarian works on, prompting expanded crop yields, decreased asset use, and further developed supportability.

GIS innovation helps with making accuracy agribusiness maps, which guide ranchers in settling on informed conclusions about planting, treatment, and irritation control.

By overlaying information layers connected with soil organization, vegetation wellbeing, and environment conditions, ranchers can carry out designated mediations to address explicit difficulties in various pieces of their fields. This combination of remote detecting and GIS adds to manageable and productive cultivating rehearses.

Metropolitan Preparation and Foundation Improvement

In the domain of metropolitan preparation and foundation improvement, remote detecting and GIS assume critical parts in social occasion and examining spatial information. Satellite symbolism gives exceptional data on metropolitan extension, land use changes, and the improvement of framework projects. GIS apparatuses work with the production of definite metropolitan guides, supporting city organizers in arriving at informed conclusions about drafting, transportation, and asset assignment.

For instance, satellite symbolism can be utilized to screen never-ending suburbia and evaluate the effect of new improvements on the general climate. GIS permits organizers to demonstrate various situations and investigate the likely outcomes of metropolitan development. This data is significant for establishing economical and tough metropolitan conditions that address the issues of developing populaces while limiting negative natural effects.

Calamity The executives and Reaction

emote detecting and GIS are instrumental in calamity the executives and reaction endeavors. During catastrophic events like seismic tremors, floods, or out of control fires, ideal and precise data is basic for planning salvage tasks, evaluating harms, and arranging recuperation endeavors. Satellite symbolism and ethereal overviews give constant information on catastrophe impacted regions, assisting specialists with pursuing informed choices.

GIS innovation supports the production of definite debacle risk maps, which feature weak regions and aid clearing arranging. Remote detecting can be utilized to screen the movement of calamities, like following the development of fierce blazes or evaluating the degree of flooding. By incorporating these advancements, crisis responders can focus on their endeavors and designate assets proficiently, at last lessening the effect of fiascos on networks.

Wellbeing and Illness Observing

Remote detecting and GIS have applications in observing general wellbeing and following the spread of illnesses. Satellite symbolism can be utilized to concentrate on natural factors that impact the predominance of infections, for example, the accessibility of water bodies that might act as favorable places for illness vectors. GIS devices help in planning illness episodes, recognizing high-risk regions, and arranging mediations to control the spread of irresistible sicknesses.

For example, the observing of vector-borne illnesses like intestinal sickness or dengue includes dissecting natural circumstances, like temperature and precipitation, to anticipate the regions generally helpless to episodes. GIS permits wellbeing specialists to overlay this data with populace information, working with designated mediations, for example, mosquito control measures and public mindfulness crusades.

Regular Asset The board

Remote detecting and GIS assume a basic part in the reasonable administration of regular assets, including water, timberlands, and minerals. Satellite symbolism can give data on changes in land cover, deforestation rates, and water quality. GIS devices help in the production of asset maps, permitting policymakers and asset administrators to settle on informed conclusions about asset extraction, protection, and land-use arranging.

With regards to water asset the board, remote detecting can screen changes in water bodies, track dry season conditions, and evaluate the effect of environmental change on water accessibility. GIS works with the combination of different information sources, empowering a thorough comprehension of the variables impacting water assets. This data is important for planning viable water the board systems that offset human necessities with natural supportability.

Military and Guard Applications

Remote detecting and GIS advancements have for quite some time been utilized in military and guard applications. Satellite symbolism gives important knowledge to checking international turns of events, surveying military framework, and arranging key tasks. GIS devices help in the examination of territory, the distinguishing proof of key areas, and the preparation of military missions.

Notwithstanding conventional guard applications, remote detecting and GIS add to catastrophe reaction in struggle zones. Satellite symbolism can be utilized to evaluate the effect of struggles on foundation and non military personnel populaces, working with compassionate guide endeavors. The mix of remote detecting and GIS improves situational mindfulness, permitting military and philanthropic associations to answer actually to intricate and dynamic circumstances.

Difficulties and Future Patterns

While remote detecting and GIS offer various advantages, there are difficulties related with their inescapable execution. High-goal satellite symbolism and high level GIS programming can be expensive, restricting access for more modest associations and agricultural nations. Furthermore, the understanding of remote detecting information requires particular information, featuring the requirement for limit building and preparing programs.

Moreover, moral contemplations, for example, protection concerns connected with the utilization of high-goal symbolism, should be tended to. Finding some kind of harmony between the advantages of these innovations and the likely dangers to protection is fundamental for mindful and moral use.

Looking forward, a few patterns are molding the fate of remote detecting and GIS applications. The improvement of little satellite heavenly bodies, headways in sensor innovation, and the rising accessibility of open-source GIS programming are making these advancements more available. The joining of computerized reasoning and AI into remote detecting and GIS work processes is likewise improving the computerization of information investigation and understanding.

8.2 Data Analytics for Land Use Change

Land use change is a dynamic and complex peculiarity impacted by different elements, including populace development, urbanization, horticultural practices, and ecological contemplations. Understanding and observing area use change are fundamental for practical turn of events, natural preservation, and successful land the executives. Information examination, with its capacity to process and dissect huge measures of information, has arisen as an integral asset in translating examples, patterns, and drivers of land use change. This article investigates the utilizations of information examination in concentrating ashore use change, underlining its importance in directing informed navigation and encouraging economical practices.

The Significance of Observing Area Use Change

Land use change envelops modifications in the manner land is used, whether through urbanization, deforestation, horticultural development, or different changes. The results of these progressions can be significant, influencing environments, biodiversity, environment examples, and human prosperity. Observing area use change is basic because of multiple factors:

Ecological Preservation: Understanding what land use changes mean for regular environments, biological systems, and biodiversity is pivotal for protection endeavors. It takes into consideration the recognizable proof of regions in danger and the advancement of methodologies to relieve negative ecological effects.

Maintainable Turn of events: Checking land use change upholds manageable advancement by giving bits of knowledge into the harmony between financial development and ecological protection. It recognizes regions reasonable for improvement and those that ought to be moderated to keep up with biological respectability.

Asset The executives: Effective administration of regular assets, including water, soil, and timberlands, depends on exact data about land use changes. Information examination supports evaluating asset accessibility, distinguishing regions inclined to debasement, and enhancing asset use.

Environmental Change Moderation: Land use change is unpredictably connected to environmental change. Checking and examining land use designs add to understanding the carbon balance, recognizing wellsprings of discharges, and creating procedures for environmental change relief.

Utilizations of Information Examination in Land Use Change

Information investigation incorporates a scope of procedures, including measurable examination, AI, and spatial demonstrating, that can be applied to different datasets for extricating significant bits of knowledge. With regards to land use change, information examination tracks down applications in different areas:

Remote Detecting and Satellite Symbolism Investigation: Remote detecting information, got through satellites or elevated stages, give an abundance of data about the World's surface. Information examination methods are applied to satellite symbolism for land cover arrangement, change recognition, and checking patterns after some time. AI calculations, for instance, can be prepared to distinguish different land cover types, like metropolitan regions, backwoods, and farming fields, from satellite symbolism.

Transient Examination: Fleeting investigation includes concentrating on changes over the long haul, which is especially pertinent with regards to land use change. Time-series information, for example, satellite symbolism caught at various stretches, can be investigated to identify patterns and examples. Information examination assists in recognizing the timing and speed of land with utilizing changes, considering a more nuanced comprehension of the drivers behind these changes.

Geospatial Investigation and Geographic Data Frameworks (GIS): Geospatial examination includes the examination of spatial information, and GIS is a useful asset for overseeing and breaking down geographic data. These innovations empower the joining of different datasets, for example, land cover maps, populace thickness, and framework, to acquire a far reaching comprehension of land use designs. GIS takes into account the making of guides that envision the spatial circulation of land use changes and their suggestions.

AI for Prescient Displaying: AI calculations can be utilized to foster prescient models for land use change. Via preparing models on authentic information, these calculations can recognize examples and connections that add to land use changes. When prepared, the models can be utilized to make expectations about future land use situations under various circumstances, helping with navigation and arranging.

Huge Information Examination: The rising accessibility of enormous and different datasets, frequently alluded to as large information, gives an open door to additional thorough investigations. Huge information investigation can process gigantic datasets, including satellite symbolism, environment information, and financial markers, to reveal complex connections and patterns connected with land use change.

Challenges in Information Examination for Land Use Change

While information examination holds extraordinary commitment in understanding and observing area use change, there are difficulties that should be tended to:

Information Quality and Accessibility: The precision and dependability of information are essential to the progress of information investigation applications. In certain districts, information might be scant or of changing quality, presenting difficulties to the advancement of exact models and examinations.

Interdisciplinary Cooperation: Powerful land use change investigation requires coordinated effort between specialists from assorted fields, including natural science, geology, software engineering, and measurements. Interdisciplinary coordinated effort is significant for creating comprehensive models that think about ecological, social, and monetary variables.

Moral Contemplations: The utilization of information examination in land use change checking raises moral contemplations connected with protection, information possession, and the likely abuse of data. Dependable information administration and moral rules are vital for address these worries.

Limit Building: Executing information examination requires a gifted labor force fit for dealing with cutting edge insightful devices and deciphering results. Limit building drives are expected to prepare experts in the interdisciplinary abilities expected for powerful land use change examination.

Contextual investigations: True Uses of Information Examination

Deforestation Checking in the Amazon Rainforest:
Information Source: Satellite symbolism from stages like Landsat and Sentinel.
Investigation Approach: AI calculations prepared on verifiable satellite symbolism to identify examples of deforestation.
Result: Recognizable proof of deforested regions, observing of unlawful logging exercises, and evaluation of the effect on biodiversity.
Metropolitan Development Forecast in Creating Urban communities:
Information Source: Satellite symbolism, populace information, and foundation maps.
Investigation Approach: Spatial displaying and AI calculations to foresee metropolitan development designs.
Result: Informed metropolitan preparation, ID of regions in danger of fast urbanization, and advancement of framework improvement.
Accuracy Agribusiness for Reasonable Cultivating:
Information Source: Satellite symbolism, climate information, and soil structure information.
Examination Approach: Combination of remote detecting information with GIS for accuracy horticulture.
Result: Further developed crop yield forecasts, advanced asset use, and manageable cultivating rehearses.
Environmental Change Effect Evaluation:
Information Source: Environment models, satellite symbolism, and financial information.
Examination Approach: Huge information investigation to break down complex cooperations between environmental change and land use change.
Result: ID of weak locales, appraisal of environmental change influences on agribusiness, and detailing of versatile systems.
Future Bearings and Developments
The field of information examination for land use change is ceaselessly developing, and a few patterns and advancements are molding its future:
Incorporation of Different Information Sources: Future applications will include the coordination of assorted information sources, including satellite symbolism, environment models, online entertainment information, and resident science inputs. Consolidating these sources will give a more complete comprehension of the elements impacting land use change.
Continuous Checking: Advances in satellite innovation and information examination are empowering ongoing observing of land use changes. This ability is significant for answering speedily to arising ecological difficulties, like unlawful logging, fierce blazes, and catastrophic events.
Reasonable simulated intelligence Models: As AI models become more complex, there is a developing accentuation on creating models that are logical and interpretable.

This is especially significant with regards to land use change, where chiefs need to comprehend the elements driving model expectations.

Resident Science and Publicly supported Information: Including the general population in information assortment through resident science drives and publicly supported information can improve the spatial and transient goal of datasets. Coordinating these contributions with customary information sources can give a more itemized and confined perspective ashore use changes.

Blockchain Innovation for Information Trustworthiness: Blockchain innovation, known for its solid and straightforward record-keeping, can be applied to guarantee the uprightness of land use information. This can address concerns connected with information altering and upgrade trust in the data utilized for navigation.

8.3 Citizen Science and Participatory Mapping

Resident science and participatory planning are imaginative methodologies that draw in people and networks in logical exploration and geographic data creation. These strategies democratize the logical cycle by including non-experts in information assortment, examination, and direction. This article investigates the ideas of resident science and participatory planning, their importance in different fields, and the extraordinary effect they have on logical exploration, natural protection, and local area strengthening.

Resident Science: Drawing in People in general in Logical Exploration

Resident science alludes to the contribution of the overall population in logical examination exercises, frequently in a joint effort with proficient researchers or logical establishments.

This cooperative methodology takes advantage of the aggregate force of people to contribute important information and bits of knowledge across assorted logical disciplines. Resident science projects differ generally, incorporating fields, for example, biology, cosmology, natural checking, biodiversity studies, and general wellbeing.

Key Qualities of Resident Science:

Inclusivity: Resident science projects are comprehensive, inviting members from different foundations, no matter what their degree of logical mastery. This inclusivity guarantees a different scope of viewpoints and commitments.

Information Assortment: Members effectively add to information assortment, either by mentioning objective facts, directing investigations, or utilizing innovation, for example, cell phones to record and submit information. This conveyed information assortment model empowers the social event of enormous datasets over expansive geographic regions.

Cooperation: Resident science projects frequently include joint effort between non-experts and researchers. This cooperative methodology cultivates shared learning, with members acquiring logical information and analysts profiting from the expanded volume of information.

Local area Commitment: Resident science projects much of the time draw in nearby networks, cultivating a feeling of responsibility and association with the logical cycle. This commitment can prompt expanded natural mindfulness and a more grounded feeling of obligation for nearby environments.

Instances of Resident Science Ventures:

eBird: A stage where birdwatchers overall contribute bird sightings, assisting researchers with following bird populaces, relocation designs, and the effect of natural changes.

Zooniverse: A web-based stage facilitating an assortment of resident science projects in fields like stargazing, science, and environment science. Members can assist with investigating information from space missions, characterize worlds, or interpret authentic archives.

Resident Climate Eyewitness Program (CWOP): People offer climate information from individual weather conditions stations, improving the exactness of nearby weather conditions conjectures and supporting environment research.

Participatory Planning: Enabling People group through Geographic Data

Participatory planning includes the cooperative production of guides that address the spatial information on a local area. It goes past customary map making by integrating nearby viewpoints, native information, and local area bits of knowledge into the planning system. Participatory planning not just fills in as an important device for picturing spatial data yet additionally enables networks to effectively participate in dynamic cycles connected with land use, asset the board, and natural preservation.

Key Qualities of Participatory Planning:

Local area Contribution: Participatory planning accentuates the dynamic association of local area individuals in making maps that mirror their insight and lived encounters. This contribution guarantees that the guides are socially applicable and precise.

Neighborhood Information Combination: The planning system incorporates nearby information, frequently went down through ages, about the scene, normal assets, and socially huge destinations. This information improves the extravagance and logical importance of the guides.

Strengthening: Participatory planning engages networks by furnishing them with a device to communicate their spatial figuring out, advocate for their necessities, and partake in dynamic cycles. It advances a granular perspective to arranging and improvement.

Asset The board: The guides made through participatory planning can be instrumental in overseeing normal assets reasonably. They give bits of knowledge into asset conveyance, utilization examples, and areas of natural significance, helping with preservation endeavors.

Instances of Participatory Planning Drives:

Local area Based Planning in Native Regions: Native people group utilize participatory planning to report conventional domains, hallowed destinations, and areas of environmental importance. These guides support land privileges backing and social protection.

OpenStreetMap: A cooperative planning stage where people and networks contribute geographic information, for example, street organizations and focal points. OpenStreetMap is utilized all around the world for calamity reaction, metropolitan preparation, and local area improvement.

Counter-Planning Activism: In cases where official guides may not precisely address nearby real factors, networks participate in counter-planning to challenge prevailing stories and promoter for their privileges. This type of planning is frequently connected with social and natural equity developments.

Cooperative energies between Resident Science and Participatory Planning

While resident science and participatory planning are particular ideas, they share normal standards and can complete one another in different ways. The combination of these methodologies makes cooperative energies that improve local area commitment, logical exploration, and dynamic cycles.

Local area Drove Ecological Checking: Joining resident science with participatory planning permits networks to gather natural information as well as spatially address their perceptions. For instance, a local area observing water quality might utilize participatory planning to feature areas of worry on a guide, giving a spatial setting to their discoveries.

Spatial Information for Navigation: Participatory planning produces spatial information that can be incorporated into logical examinations directed through resident science drives. This coordination upgrades the lavishness of datasets and gives a more far reaching comprehension of natural changes.

Local area Strengthening through Information: Both resident science and participatory planning engage networks by permitting them to add to the age of information effectively. This feeling of responsibility and inclusion cultivates a more profound association between local area individuals and the issues they are tending to.

Backing and Strategy Impact: The mix of resident science information and participatory guides can be a strong promotion device. Networks can utilize these assets to impact approaches, show the effect of natural changes, and backer for supportable practices.

Contextual analyses: Cooperative Methodologies in real life

Portable Innovation for Local area Drove Ecological Observing:

Area: The Peruvian Amazon.

Drive: Native people group utilize cell phones to gather information on deforestation, water quality, and biodiversity. The gathered information are then coordinated into participatory guides, illuminating area use arranging and supporting backing endeavors for timberland preservation.

Metropolitan Preparation through Local area Planning:
Area: Casual settlements in Nairobi, Kenya.

Drive: Occupants of casual settlements utilize participatory planning to record their areas, including foundation, water sources, and medical care offices. The guides act as a reason for local area drove metropolitan arranging drives, upholding for further developed administrations and foundation.

Resident Science for Coral Reef Protection:

Area: The Incomparable Hindrance Reef, Australia.

Drive: Jumpers and swimmers add to resident science endeavors by gathering information on coral wellbeing, marine life, and ecological circumstances. This information is then used to make maps representing the situation with various reef regions, supporting protection procedures and the executives choices.

Difficulties and Contemplations

While resident science and participatory planning offer huge advantages, a few difficulties and contemplations should be addressed for these ways to deal with find lasting success:

Information Quality and Normalization: Guaranteeing the quality and dependability of information gathered by non-experts is a key test. Normalizing information assortment conventions, giving preparation, and executing quality control measures are fundamental.

Inclusivity and Portrayal: Endeavors ought to be made to guarantee that resident science and participatory planning drives are comprehensive and agent of assorted networks. This incorporates resolving issues of access, social awareness, and language boundaries.

Moral Contemplations: Regarding the privileges and points of view of networks engaged with these drives is significant. Moral contemplations incorporate getting educated assent, safeguarding native information, and guaranteeing that information use lines up with the upsides of the local area.

Limit Building: Building the limit of local area individuals and volunteers is fundamental for the outcome of these drives. This includes giving preparation in information assortment, planning devices, and grasping the more extensive setting of the ventures.

Combination with Formal Dynamic Cycles: To augment influence, resident science and participatory planning drives ought to look to coordinate their results with formal dynamic cycles. This includes making channels for the consideration of local area created information in legislative approaches and advancement plans.

Chapter 9

Challenges And Future Prospects

The 21st century has introduced a period of extraordinary mechanical, social, and ecological changes, carrying with it a heap of difficulties and valuable open doors. From the ascent of computerized reasoning to the worldwide effect of environmental change, social orders all over the planet are wrestling with complex issues that request creative arrangements. This paper investigates the diverse difficulties looked by humankind in the current day and digs into the potential future possibilities that might shape our aggregate predetermination.

1. **Innovative Difficulties:**
1. **Man-made reasoning and Robotization:**
   The fast headway of man-made brainpower (simulated intelligence) and computerization presents critical difficulties to the worldwide labor force. As machines become progressively fit for performing complex errands, the anxiety toward work uprooting and monetary imbalance poses a potential threat. Finding some kind of harmony between mechanical advancement and cultural prosperity turns into a basic test.

   Also, moral worries encompassing artificial intelligence, for example, predisposition in calculations and the potential for independent direction, request cautious thought. As we incorporate these innovations into our regular routines, inquiries regarding security, responsibility, and the moral utilization of computer based intelligence should be addressed to guarantee an amicable conjunction among people and machines.
2. **Network safety:**

The interconnected idea of the computerized age has presented social orders to new weaknesses. Network protection challenges, going from information breaks to ransomware assaults, compromise individual protection as well as public safety.

As innovation advances, so do the strategies of cybercriminals, requiring consistent development in online protection measures.

The insurance of basic framework, touchy data, and individual information has turned into a central concern. States, organizations, and people the same should team up to foster hearty network protection structures that can endure the always developing complexity of digital dangers.

II. Natural Difficulties:

1. Environmental Change:

Maybe the most squeezing challenge within recent memory, environmental change is modifying the planet's biological systems and presenting existential dangers to innumerable species, including people. Increasing worldwide temperatures, outrageous climate occasions, and liquefying ice covers are only a couple of signs of the intricate trap of issues related with environmental change.

Moderating and adjusting to environmental change requires global participation, imaginative advancements, and an essential change in cultural mentalities toward supportability. Changing to environmentally friendly power sources, executing green innovations, and cultivating protection endeavors are basic strides toward an additional practical and strong future.

2. Biodiversity Misfortune:

The deficiency of biodiversity is another natural test that frequently remains closely connected with environmental change. Human exercises like deforestation, environment obliteration, and contamination add to the fast decay of plant and creature species. The outcomes of biodiversity misfortune are broad, influencing biological systems, food security, and human wellbeing.

Protection endeavors, environment rebuilding, and maintainable asset the board are fundamental parts of tending to biodiversity misfortune. The test lies in tracking down a sensitive harmony between monetary turn of events and natural safeguarding to guarantee the prosperity of both present and people in the future.

III. Social and Social Difficulties:

1. Imbalance:

Regardless of mechanical progressions and expanded worldwide network, financial imbalance stays an inescapable issue. Differences in pay, training, and admittance to essential assets persevere on a worldwide scale. Crossing over these holes requires financial strategies that focus on fair circulation as well as a change in cultural perspectives toward inclusivity.

Training assumes a vital part in breaking the pattern of neediness and disparity. Putting resources into school systems that give equivalent open doors to all, paying little heed to financial foundation, is fundamental for building an additional fair and prosperous world.

2. **Worldwide Wellbeing Pandemics:**

The episode of the Coronavirus pandemic featured the interconnectedness of the worldwide local area and the weaknesses of general wellbeing frameworks.

Arising irresistible sicknesses, anti-infection obstruction, and other wellbeing challenges require facilitated global reactions and vigorous medical care foundations.

Reinforcing worldwide wellbeing frameworks, putting resources into innovative work, and advancing wellbeing value are key parts of tending to current and future pandemics. The examples gained from the Coronavirus emergency highlight the significance of readiness and participation notwithstanding worldwide wellbeing dangers.

IV. Financial Difficulties:

1. **Globalization and Exchange:**
   While globalization has achieved expanded financial relationship, it has likewise brought about difficulties like exchange irregular characteristics, protectionism, and the re-appropriating of occupations. Finding some kind of harmony between the advantages of worldwide exchange and the need to safeguard home-grown enterprises and laborers represents a complex monetary test.
   The ascent of patriot opinions in certain areas of the planet highlights the pressure among globalization and the longing for monetary independence. Creating exchange arrangements that advance reasonableness, inclusivity, and supportable improvement is pivotal for exploring the monetary difficulties of the 21st hundred years.
2. **Financial Strength and Versatility:**

The powerful idea of the worldwide economy, combined with unanticipated disturbances like the Coronavirus pandemic, features the significance of monetary versatility and flexibility. Conventional models of financial development and improvement might should be reexamined to guarantee an additional supportable and comprehensive future.

Putting resources into development, encouraging business venture, and advancing a different and talented labor force are key systems for building monetary strength. States and organizations should team up to make deft and versatile monetary frameworks that can endure shocks and vulnerabilities.

V. Future Possibilities:

1. **Mechanical Development and Cooperation:**
   Regardless of the difficulties presented by mechanical headways, there is

tremendous potential for advancement to resolve squeezing worldwide issues. Joint effort between legislatures, organizations, and research foundations can outfit the force of innovation for everyone's benefit. Drives zeroed in on mindful man-made intelligence improvement, sustainable power, and advancement clinical innovations hold guarantee for molding a positive future.

2. **Economical Turn of events:**

The quest for maintainable improvement offers a pathway to address ecological, social, and financial difficulties at the same time. Putting resources into green innovations, advancing roundabout economies, and embracing eco-accommodating practices can add to a more reasonable future. Peaceful accords and responsibilities, like the Unified Countries Practical Improvement Objectives, give a system to aggregate activity toward an additional impartial and naturally cognizant world.

3. **Social and Social Change:**

Building an all the more and comprehensive society requires a change in friendly and social standards. Embracing variety, advancing fairness, and cultivating sympathy are fundamental for conquering well established issues like disparity and separation. Training and mindfulness missions can assume a vital part in molding a worldwide mentality that values empathy and collaboration.

4. **Worldwide Administration and Collaboration:**

5. Tending to difficulties on a worldwide scale requires successful administration designs and global participation. Reinforcing worldwide establishments, advancing discretionary exchange, and cultivating joint effort between countries are fundamental for handling issues that rise above borders, for example, environmental change, pandemics, and digital dangers. The improvement of a more interconnected and helpful world request is a critical possibility for what's in store.

9.1 Emerging Issues in Land Use Conservation

Land use protection has turned into an inexorably basic part of feasible advancement as human populaces develop, and natural difficulties heighten. Arising issues in land use protection request our consideration and key endeavors to figure out some kind of harmony between monetary turn of events and the safeguarding of normal assets. In this exposition, we will investigate key difficulties and open doors related with contemporary land use protection, analyzing the ramifications for biodiversity, biological systems, and the prosperity of people in the future.

1. **Urbanization and Environment Discontinuity:**

1. **Never-ending suburbia:**

The quick extension of metropolitan regions, driven by populace development and industrialization, has prompted broad endless suburbia. This peculiarity infringes upon regular environments, changing over perfect scenes into substantial wildernesses. As urban communities grow, the normal environments that offer fundamental biological types of assistance are upset, prompting living space misfortune, discontinuity, and a decrease in biodiversity.

Adjusting the requirement for metropolitan advancement with the protection of green spaces and untamed life environments requires inventive metropolitan preparation. Carrying out feasible metropolitan plan works on, making green passages, and laying out safeguarded metropolitan wild regions are possible answers for alleviate the adverse consequences of endless suburbia.

2. **Framework Advancement:**

Huge scope framework projects, like streets, dams, and mining tasks, frequently bring about territory annihilation and environment debasement. These improvements not just straightforwardly influence the widely varied vegetation dwelling in the impacted regions yet in addition add to long haul ecological results, including soil disintegration, water contamination, and modified hydrological designs.

Supportable foundation improvement includes consolidating natural effect evaluations, taking into account elective courses or plans to limit biological disturbance, and executing alleviation measures. Drawing in with nearby networks and partners in the arranging system can assist with finding some kind of harmony between advancement objectives and protection needs.

II. Farming Practices and Land Change:

1. **Serious Agribusiness:**
Current farming practices, portrayed by monoculture, weighty pesticide use, and huge scope water system, have prompted critical natural difficulties. Soil corruption, loss of biodiversity, and water contamination are ramifications of escalated farming. The transformation of normal territories into agrarian land further compounds these issues.

Progressing towards reasonable and regenerative horticultural practices is vital for alleviating the ecological effect of food creation. Agroecological approaches, natural cultivating, and accuracy horticulture can upgrade rural manageability while limiting mischief to biological systems. Supporting limited scope ranchers and advancing dependable land stewardship are fundamental parts of an economical food framework.

2. **Land Use Change:**

The transformation of regular scenes into horticultural land, especially for cash harvests and animals cultivating, represents a danger to biodiversity and biological system wellbeing. Deforestation, wetland waste, and change of regular meadows add to the deficiency of basic territories and the removal of local species.

Executing arrangements that advance reasonable land use works on, safeguarding environmentally touchy regions, and boosting agroforestry and preservation agreeable cultivating techniques are fundamental systems. Building mindfulness among ranchers and the overall population about the significance of keeping up with normal biological systems for long haul farming efficiency is likewise basic.

III. Environmental Change and Land Protection:

1. **Modified Environments:**
Environmental change represents a multi-layered challenge to land use preservation. Climbing temperatures, changing precipitation examples, and outrageous climate occasions can adjust biological systems, making them less versatile to natural stressors. Changes in vegetation zones, disturbances to transitory examples, and the spread of obtrusive species are undeniably connected to environmental change.

Versatile land the executives procedures are expected to address the effects of environmental change on biological systems. This might include reforestation endeavors, the foundation of environment tough passages for untamed life movement, and the protection of regular carbon sinks like timberlands and wetlands.

2. **Ocean Level Ascent and Beach front Disintegration:**

Environmental change-actuated ocean level ascent compromises seaside biological systems and the networks that rely upon them. Beach front disintegration, saltwater interruption into freshwater frameworks, and the deficiency of important wetlands are among the outcomes of rising ocean levels. Safeguarding beach front territories isn't just urgent for biodiversity yet in addition for buffering against the effects of outrageous climate occasions.

Executing waterfront protection and reclamation projects, like mangrove reforestation and the making of counterfeit reefs, can assist with alleviating the impacts of ocean level ascent. Incorporating environment variation measures into beach front improvement plans is fundamental to guarantee the drawn out supportability of waterfront biological systems.

IV. Native Land Freedoms and Preservation:

1. **Dislodging and Social Effect:**
   Land use protection endeavors frequently meet with the regions customarily possessed by native networks. Dislodging coming about because of preservation drives can have significant social, social, and monetary effects on these networks. The deficiency of genealogical grounds and disturbance of conventional practices can prompt a deficiency of biodiversity information and compound social disparities.
   Regarding and perceiving native land freedoms is essential to compelling protection. Cooperative methodologies that include native networks in dynamic cycles, consolidate customary biological information, and backing maintainable land the board practices can add to both preservation objectives and the prosperity of native people groups.

2. **Protection and Jobs:**

   Native people group frequently assume a pivotal part in maintainable land the executives and biodiversity protection. Their conventional practices, established in a profound comprehension of nearby biological systems, add to the versatility of regular natural surroundings. Nonetheless, preservation strategies that don't represent the necessities and freedoms of native networks can prompt struggles and subvert protection endeavors.

   Executing people group based protection drives that enable native networks, maintain their freedoms, and perceive their commitments is fundamental. Cooperative protection models that coordinate customary information with logical methodologies can prompt more powerful and comprehensive land use preservation.

   V. Arising Advancements in Land Use Protection:

1. **Geospatial Innovation:**
   Progressions in geospatial innovation, including satellite symbolism and remote detecting, have altered land use checking and protection endeavors. These devices give constant information ashore cover changes, deforestation, and environment fracture, empowering more exact and ideal mediations.
   Coordinating geospatial innovation into preservation arranging considers proof based navigation and the ID of need regions for assurance. The utilization of Geographic Data Framework (GIS) planning can upgrade how we might interpret scene elements and backing protection systems at neighborhood, local, and worldwide scales.

2. **Blockchain and Preservation Money:**

Blockchain innovation can possibly change preservation finance by giving straightforward and recognizable instruments to subsidizing protection projects. Through tokenization, blockchain can empower people and associations to put straightforwardly in protection drives, guaranteeing that assets are dispensed productively and that the effect of speculations is quantifiable.

Investigating imaginative monetary models, for example, installments for environment administrations and biodiversity balances, can use blockchain innovation to boost landowners and networks to take part in protection endeavors. This approach adjusts financial interests to natural stewardship, making a more feasible and decentralized subsidizing scene for land use preservation.

VI. Local area Commitment and Ecological Equity:

1. **Comprehensive Navigation:**
   Effective land use protection requires the dynamic support of nearby networks. Generally speaking, preservation drives have flopped because of hierarchical methodologies that disregard the requirements and viewpoints of those straightforwardly impacted. Comprehensive dynamic cycles that consolidate nearby information, social qualities, and local area goals are fundamental for encouraging a feeling of pride and obligation.
   Enabling nearby networks to effectively take part in protection arranging and execution guarantees that drives are customized to the particular requirements of the area. This participatory methodology can improve the viability and maintainability of preservation endeavors.
2. **Natural Equity:**

   Land use choices can excessively affect defenseless and underestimated networks. Natural equity concerns, including inconsistent circulation of ecological advantages and weights, should be addressed to guarantee fair and impartial protection results. By and large, hindered networks have borne the brunt of natural debasement and have had restricted admittance to the advantages of protection.

   Upholding for ecological equity includes perceiving and tending to the social imbalances implanted in land use arrangements. Cooperative endeavors with local area pioneers, grassroots associations, and policymakers are important to formulate preservation techniques that focus on decency and inclusivity.

9.2 Climate Change and Land Use Interactions

The multifaceted dance between environmental change and land use has arisen as a characterizing challenge within recent memory, forming biological systems, affecting biodiversity, and impacting the livelihoods of networks around the world. As human exercises modify scenes and delivery ozone depleting substances, the World's environment answers with shifts in temperature, precipitation examples, and outrageous climate occasions. This paper investigates the complicated communications between environmental change and land use, revealing insight into the results, difficulties, and potential arrangements that emerge from this cooperative relationship.

1. **Land Use Practices and Ozone depleting substance Outflows:**
1. **Deforestation and Carbon Sequestration:**

Deforestation, driven by farming extension, logging, and foundation advancement, contributes fundamentally to the arrival of carbon dioxide into the air. Woodlands go about as carbon sinks, engrossing and putting away a lot of carbon through photosynthesis.

At the point when trees are chopped down or consumed, the put away carbon is delivered, increasing the nursery impact and adding to a worldwide temperature alteration.

Maintainable woods the executives rehearses, afforestation drives, and arrangements pointed toward lessening deforestation are urgent for relieving fossil fuel byproducts. Reforestation endeavors sequester carbon as well as reestablish environments, improve biodiversity, and backing nearby networks.

2. **Horticulture and Methane Outflows:**

Horticultural exercises, especially animals cultivating and rice development, are significant wellsprings of methane emanations. Methane, a powerful ozone depleting substance, is delivered during the stomach related cycles of ruminant creatures and from overflowed rice paddies. Serious cultivating practices and enormous scope domesticated animals tasks fuel these discharges.

Carrying out feasible rural practices, for example, agroecology and regenerative cultivating, can decrease methane emanations. Also, progressions in feed added substances for domesticated animals and further developed rice development strategies can add to bringing down the natural effect of agribusiness.

II. Input Circles and Enhancing Impacts:

1. **Permafrost Defrost and Arrival of Methane:**

The defrosting of permafrost, a frozen layer of soil in Cold locales, represents a huge criticism circle with regards to environmental change. As permafrost defrosts, natural matter recently safeguarded in the frozen soil decays, delivering a lot of methane and carbon dioxide. These strong ozone depleting substances further add to warming temperatures, making a self-supporting cycle.

Moderating permafrost defrost requires complete endeavors to lessen by and large ozone harming substance emanations. Progressing to environmentally friendly power, restricting deforestation, and taking on manageable land use rehearses are fundamental parts of tending to this enhancing impact.

2. **Sea Fermentation and Coral Reefs:**

Land use rehearses, like deforestation and modern exercises, add to expanded carbon dioxide levels in the climate. A huge part of this overabundance carbon dioxide is consumed by the world's seas, prompting sea fermentation. Fermentation represents an extreme danger to marine biological systems, especially coral reefs.

Coral reefs, significant for biodiversity and fisheries, are exceptionally delicate to changes in sea science. Dying occasions, strengthened by warming ocean temperatures, further pressure coral reefs.

Saving these biological systems requires a double methodology: diminishing fossil fuel byproducts to slow fermentation and executing preservation measures to shield coral reefs from extra stressors.

III. Influences on Biological systems and Biodiversity:

1. **Moving Living spaces and Reach Changes:**
The changing environment prompts shifts in temperature and precipitation designs, modifying the geographic circulation of biological systems. Species familiar with explicit environment conditions might track down their natural surroundings unacceptable, prompting relocation or, in most pessimistic scenarios, eradication. This peculiarity is apparent in the relocation of plant and creature species toward higher heights or scopes. Successful protection techniques should think about the powerful idea of environments. Laying out safeguarded regions, making untamed life halls, and helping species in their movement are fundamental measures to save biodiversity despite environment prompted living space changes.

2. **Outrageous Climate Occasions and Living space Obliteration:**

The expansion in recurrence and power of outrageous climate occasions, like tropical storms, fierce blazes, and floods, devastatingly affects environments and scenes. Fast and serious fierce blazes, for example, can prompt the annihilation of woods and other normal natural surroundings, bringing about territory fracture and loss of biodiversity.

and variation procedures are critical for biological systems confronting the effects of outrageous climate occasions. These may incorporate controlled consumes to decrease rapidly spreading fire gambles, reforestation endeavors, and the making of support zones to safeguard weak environments.

IV. Practical Land The executives and Variation Methodologies:

1. **Environment Based Variation:**
   Environment based variation includes outfitting the flexibility of regular biological systems to adapt to the effects of environmental change. This approach stresses the protection and reclamation of environments, perceiving their part in controlling environment, offering fundamental types of assistance, and supporting biodiversity.
   Instances of biological system based transformation incorporate the reclamation of mangrove woodlands to shield shorelines from storm floods and ocean level ascent or the conservation of wetlands to moderate flooding. Coordinating these techniques into land use arranging improves the general flexibility of networks and environments.

2. **Environment Shrewd Farming:**

   Environment shrewd farming addresses a methodology that tends to the exchange between environmental change and land use with regards to food creation. This approach underscores economical and strong agrarian practices that add to both environment relief and transformation. Procedures incorporate accuracy cultivating, agroforestry, and the utilization of environment strong harvest assortments.

   Supporting ranchers in taking on environment shrewd works on, giving admittance to important advances, and coordinating these methodologies into rural strategies add to building a more reasonable and versatile food framework.

   V. Worldwide Collaboration and Strategy Systems:

1. **Paris Understanding and NDCs:**
   The Paris Understanding, a milestone worldwide accord, looks to restrict an Earth-wide temperature boost to well under 2 degrees Celsius above pre-modern levels. Broadly Resolved Commitments (NDCs) frame every country's responsibilities to diminish ozone depleting substance outflows and adjust to the effects of environmental change.
   Viable execution of the Paris Understanding and aggressive NDCs is fundamental for tending to the mind boggling interaction between environmental change and land use. This includes worldwide participation, monetary help for emerging countries, and the combination of environment contemplations into land use strategies.

2. **REDD+ and Woodland Preservation:**

   Lessening Discharges from Deforestation and Woods Debasement (REDD+) is a component intended to boost woodland protection by giving monetary prizes to nations that decrease emanations from deforestation and improve backwoods carbon stocks. This drive perceives the essential job of timberlands in relieving environmental change.

Fortifying and extending REDD+ drives, alongside tending to the drivers of deforestation, add to reasonable land use rehearses. This incorporates advancing local area based backwoods the executives, authorizing hostile to deforestation regulations, and supporting elective vocations for networks reliant upon timberland assets.

VI. Public Mindfulness and Training:

1. Environment Education:

Successful activity on environmental change and land use cooperations requires a very much educated and drew in broad daylight. Environment proficiency, including a comprehension of the study of environmental change, its effects, and expected arrangements, is significant for cultivating public help and driving individual and aggregate activity.

Instructive projects, mindfulness missions, and correspondence techniques assume an imperative part in building environment education. Engaged and informed residents are bound to help strategies that advance feasible land use practices and promoter for foundational change.

9.3 Potential Solutions and Mitigation Strategies

As mankind wrestles with complex difficulties, for example, environmental change, ecological debasement, and social imbalances, the requirement for creative arrangements and powerful alleviation systems turns out to be progressively obvious. This paper investigates possible arrangements and moderation systems across different spaces, stressing the interconnectedness of these difficulties and the significance of all encompassing ways to deal with encourage a supportable and strong future.

1. Environmental Change Moderation:

1. Change to Sustainable power:

One of the essential supporters of environmental change is the dependence on petroleum products for energy. Progressing to environmentally friendly power sources, for example, sun oriented, wind, and hydropower, is a central stage toward decreasing ozone depleting substance discharges. Legislatures, organizations, and people assume basic parts in supporting and putting resources into sustainable power foundation.

Policymakers can boost environmentally friendly power reception through appropriations, tax breaks, and administrative systems that support the advancement of clean energy projects. Furthermore, innovative work endeavors zeroed in on propelling energy stockpiling innovations and working on the productivity of environmentally friendly power frameworks are fundamental for a feasible energy change.

2. **Practical Transportation:**

The transportation area is a significant wellspring of fossil fuel byproducts, principally because of the inescapable utilization of petroleum derivative controlled vehicles. Advancing maintainable transportation choices, like electric vehicles, public travel, and cycling, can essentially diminish emanations. Interests in open transportation foundation and the advancement of electric vehicle charging networks add to the reception of cleaner transportation options.

Impetuses for electric vehicle buys, eco-friendliness principles, and metropolitan arranging that focuses on walkability and public travel openness are essential parts of a thorough way to deal with manageable transportation.

II. Preservation and Biological system Insurance:

1. **Reforestation and Afforestation:**
Backwoods assume a urgent part in sequestering carbon dioxide and supporting biodiversity. Reforestation drives include establishing trees in regions that have been deforested, while afforestation includes establishing trees in regions that were not recently forested. These practices add to carbon catch, environment rebuilding, and the safeguarding of biological system administrations.

Legislatures, natural associations, and networks can work together for huge scope reforestation and afforestation projects. Drives that include neighborhood networks in tree planting, guaranteeing the utilization of local species, and giving impetuses to feasible land the board rehearses improve the adequacy of these endeavors.

2. **Economical Land Use and Agribusiness:**

Supportable land use rehearses center around limiting ecological effect while addressing human necessities. Executing agroecological approaches, like natural cultivating, permaculture, and agroforestry, assists monitor with ruining, decrease water utilization, and breaking point the utilization of engineered inputs. Besides, shielding normal living spaces from change to farming area helps safeguard biodiversity.

Policymakers can uphold feasible farming through endowments, instructive projects, and guidelines that advance harmless to the ecosystem rehearses. Shoppers likewise assume a part by picking items from organizations that focus on feasible and moral cultivating strategies.

III. Round Economy and Waste Administration:

1. **Round Economy Practices:**
   The direct "take, make, arrange" model of utilization adds to asset consumption and natural contamination. Progressing to a roundabout economy, where items are intended for life span, recyclability, and reuse, decreases the natural effect of assembling and utilization.
   Legislatures can boost round economy rehearses through approaches that empower item toughness, reusing foundation improvement, and broadened maker obligation. Organizations can embrace round plans of action, like item as-a-administration and reclaim programs, to limit squander and boost asset proficiency.
2. **Effective Waste Administration:**

   Legitimate waste administration is fundamental for relieving natural contamination and diminishing the carbon impression related with garbage removal. Reusing, treating the soil, and waste-to-energy innovations are essential parts of productive waste administration frameworks.

   Public mindfulness crusades, civil reusing projects, and interest in cutting edge squander handling advances add to viable waste administration. Coordinated effort between legislatures, organizations, and networks is significant for creating thorough waste decrease and reusing systems.

   IV. Social and Monetary Arrangements:

1. **Social Value and Incorporation:**
   Addressing social imbalances is essential to building a manageable and strong society. Arrangements that advance comprehensive monetary development, admittance to instruction, and social security nets add to lessening inconsistencies and improving by and large cultural prosperity.
   Socially capable strategic policies, variety and consideration drives, and local area commitment programs are fundamental for encouraging a more fair society. Coordinated effort between legislatures, organizations, and common society associations is essential for establishing a climate where everybody has the chance to flourish.
2. **Green Positions and Development:**

   Putting resources into green advances and ventures adds to natural maintainability as well as invigorates monetary development and occupation creation. The progress to a green economy includes creating and executing inventive innovations, like environmentally friendly power frameworks, energy-proficient foundation, and manageable horticulture rehearses.

   State run administrations can uphold the development of green enterprises through innovative work financing, charge motivators, and arrangements that advance economical strategic approaches. Schooling and preparing programs that furnish the labor force with the abilities required for green positions are likewise fundamental for a fruitful change.

V. Worldwide Collaboration and Administration:

1. **Worldwide Environment Arrangements:**
   Environmental change is a worldwide test that requires composed global endeavors. Arrangements like the Paris Understanding give a structure to nations to focus on emanation decrease targets and environment strength measures. Reinforcing and growing such arrangements are pivotal for accomplishing significant advancement in the battle against environmental change.
   Global participation includes monetary help for non-industrial countries, innovation move, and cooperative exploration drives. Tact and multilateral talks assume a focal part in encouraging a common obligation to tending to worldwide difficulties.

2. **Practical Improvement Objectives (SDGs):**

   The Unified Countries Practical Improvement Objectives incorporate an extensive arrangement of targets tending to social, financial, and ecological components of maintainability. Accomplishing these objectives includes an aggregate work to end neediness, safeguard the planet, and guarantee flourishing for all.

   Legislatures, organizations, and common society associations can adjust their systems to the SDGs to add to worldwide manageability. Revealing systems, for example, the SDG Compass, help associations in coordinating feasible practices into their activities and estimating their effect.

Chapter 10

Ethical Considerations In Land Use Conservation

Land use preservation, an imperative part of reasonable turn of events, includes complex choices that shape the connection between human social orders and the regular habitat. In exploring this territory, moral contemplations assume a urgent part in guaranteeing the dependable and evenhanded utilization of land assets. This paper dives into the moral components of land use preservation, investigating the standards, difficulties, and potential arrangements that guide our communication with the climate.

1. **Regard for Natural Worth:**
1. **Innate Worth of Nature:**
   Moral contemplations in land use protection start with perceiving the characteristic worth of nature. This viewpoint, established in ecological morals, places that nature has innate worth autonomous of its instrumental worth to people. Recognizing the natural worth of biological systems and biodiversity highlights the ethical basic to protect them for people in the future.
   Preservation strategies and practices ought to be directed by a profound regard for the inborn worth of normal elements. This includes moving past a utilitarian perspective on nature as an asset to be taken advantage of and embracing an ethic that focuses on the prospering of biological systems for the wellbeing of their own.
2. **Non-Human-centric Morals:**

Non-human-centric moral systems challenge the human-centric view that places human interests at the focal point of moral contemplations. Biocentrism, for instance, stretches out moral thought to every living being, underscoring the interconnectedness and reliance of life. Likewise, ecocentrism stretches out moral remaining to biological systems overall.

Embracing non-human-centric morals in land use preservation includes perceiving the privileges of non-human substances and integrating their prosperity into dynamic cycles. This change in context is urgent for encouraging a more amicable connection among people and the regular world.

II. Native Privileges and Nearby People group:

1. **Acknowledgment of Native Information:**

   Native people groups, frequently the stewards of biodiverse scenes, have rich natural information that has supported different biological systems for ages. Moral land use protection requires the acknowledgment and regard of Native information frameworks, which offer significant experiences into reasonable asset the board and biodiversity conservation.

   Cooperative protection endeavors ought to include significant commitment with Native people group, recognizing their privileges to land and assets. Integrating Native information into land use arranging improves the adequacy of preservation drives as well as maintains the standards of equity and regard for social variety.

2. **Free, Earlier, and Informed Assent (FPIC):**

The guideline of Free, Earlier, and Informed Assent (FPIC) is vital to moral land use preservation, especially in regions possessed by Native people groups. FPIC guarantees that networks reserve the option to arrive at conclusions about ventures or arrangements that might influence their territories, assets, or prosperity. Getting educated assent is a foundation of moral commitment with nearby networks.

States, organizations, and protection associations should focus on straightforward and comprehensive dynamic cycles that regard the independence of Native people group. Regarding FPIC isn't just a moral goal yet additionally a lawful commitment, as perceived by peaceful accords and shows.

III. Natural Equity and Value:

1. **Distributional Equity:**

   Land use choices can excessively influence different gatherings, prompting ecological treacheries. Distributional equity in land use preservation requires even-handed admittance to natural advantages and the fair conveyance of ecological weights. Defenseless and underestimated networks shouldn't bear a lopsided portion of the unfortunate results of protection endeavors.

   Moral land use protection includes directing intensive effect evaluations to recognize expected disparities and carrying out arrangements that address ecological treacheries. Guaranteeing that the advantages of preservation are shared fairly adds to an all the more and comprehensive way to deal with land the board.

2. **Financial Contemplations and Jobs:**

Adjusting preservation objectives with the financial necessities of neighborhood networks is a moral goal. Numerous people group rely upon regular assets for their occupations, and protection strategies should consider the possible effect on positions, pay, and conventional lifestyles.

Executing reasonable land the board works on, supporting elective occupations, and consolidating the points of view of nearby networks in dynamic cycles are fundamental moral contemplations. This approach perceives the interconnectedness of natural preservation and human prosperity.

IV. Moral Difficulties in Preservation Procedures:

1. **Preservation versus Advancement Quandary:**
   One of the moral difficulties in land use preservation emerges from the pressure between protection objectives and monetary turn of events. Adjusting the requirement for monetary development with the basic to safeguard biodiversity and biological systems requires cautious thought and moral direction.
   Moral arrangements include embracing manageable advancement rehearses that limit natural effect, integrating protection into improvement arranging, and looking for shared benefit situations where financial development coincides with biological safeguarding. This requires a shift away from survey protection and improvement as totally unrelated objectives.

2. **Protection Initiated Dislodging:**

Preservation drives, while fundamental for safeguarding biological systems, can some of the time lead to the dislodging of nearby networks. Moral worries emerge when preservation endeavors bring about the infringement of common freedoms, especially the option to lodging, occupation, and social practices.

Relieving the effect of preservation instigated removal includes focusing on the privileges and prosperity of impacted networks. Consolidating the viewpoints of nearby networks in the preparation and execution of protection projects, giving fair pay, and investigating local area based preservation models are moral techniques to address this test.

V. Moral Systems for Direction:

1. **Utilitarian Morals:**
   Utilitarian morals gauge the general prosperity and joy produced by a specific activity. With regards to land use preservation, utilitarian contemplations include assessing the results of protection choices on environments, biodiversity, and human prosperity.
   Utilitarian systems can direct choices that amplify generally ecological and social advantages. Notwithstanding, challenges emerge in precisely evaluating the

assorted and some of the time abstract qualities related with biological systems and social scenes.

2. **Deontological Morals:**

3.   Deontological morals, established in obligation and moral standards, can illuminate land use preservation choices in light of characteristic qualities and freedoms. This approach accentuates adherence to moral standards, for example, regarding the innate worth of nature and perceiving the freedoms of neighborhood networks.

Deontological systems give a principled establishment to moral land use protection. Be that as it may, difficulties might emerge in accommodating clashing obligations and deciding generally material moral standards.

VI. Moral Contemplations in Arising Advancements:

1. **Biotechnology and Hereditary Designing:**
Propels in biotechnology and hereditary designing proposition imaginative apparatuses for protection, like quality altering for species safeguarding. Notwithstanding, moral contemplations incorporate the likely unseen side-effects, natural effects, and the ethical status of hereditarily adjusted creatures.

Moral land use preservation implies cautious examination of the dangers and advantages of biotechnological mediations. Open and comprehensive exchanges with partners, moral oversight, and adherence to prudent standards are fundamental for mindful utilization of these advances.

2. **Blockchain and Preservation Money:**

Blockchain innovation, with its straightforward and decentralized record framework, can possibly change preservation finance. In any case, moral contemplations incorporate information protection, evenhanded conveyance of advantages, and guaranteeing that blockchain applications line up with preservation objectives.

Moral utilization of blockchain in preservation finance requires hearty administration systems, adherence to protection guidelines, and guaranteeing that neighborhood networks are not minimized in benefit-sharing game plans. Straightforwardness and responsibility are vital in keeping up with moral guidelines.

VII. Instruction and Public Mindfulness:

1. **Natural Schooling:**
Natural schooling assumes a significant part in encouraging moral mindfulness and capable way of behaving towards land use protection. Teaching general society about the interconnectedness of biological systems, the

significance of biodiversity, and the moral contemplations engaged with preservation choices enables people to pursue informed decisions.

Incorporating ecological morals into formal training educational programs, advancing public mindfulness missions, and utilizing computerized stages for natural schooling add to building an all the more morally cognizant society.

2. **City Commitment and Backing:**

Moral land use preservation requires the dynamic support of residents in dynamic cycles. Urban commitment and support empower people and networks to voice their interests, add to strategy conversations, and consider chiefs responsible.

Making spaces for public interest, supporting grassroots associations, and encouraging a culture of ecological stewardship are moral goals. Educated and drawn in residents are fundamental for driving moral land use choices at neighborhood, public, and worldwide levels.

10.1 Balancing Human Needs and Conservation Goals

The transaction between human requirements and preservation objectives addresses a sensitive difficult exercise, requiring cautious thought of ecological manageability, social value, and monetary feasibility. As the worldwide populace proceeds to develop, and formative tensions strengthen, tracking down an agreeable balance between addressing the necessities of human social orders and protecting the planet's natural respectability turns out to be progressively basic. This exposition investigates the multi-layered difficulties and potential arrangements related with adjusting human necessities and preservation objectives, looking at the moral, social, and natural elements of this complicated interaction.

1. **The Moral Objective:**
1. **Characteristic Worth of Nature:**
   Perceiving the characteristic worth of nature shapes the moral starting point for adjusting human requirements and protection objectives. This point of view, established in ecological morals, affirms that nature has inborn worth regardless of its utility to people. Embracing the inborn worth of biological systems and biodiversity lays out an ethical basic to safeguard and save the normal world.

   Moral direction includes moving past a simply utilitarian perspective on nature as an asset for human double-dealing and recognizing the inherent worth of environments, species, and scenes. This acknowledgment makes way for moral land use rehearses that consider the prosperity of both human and non-human substances.

2. **Intergenerational Value:**

Offsetting human necessities with preservation objectives requires a guarantee to intergenerational value, guaranteeing that current activities don't think twice about prosperity of people in the future.

Moral contemplations request that we be stewards of the planet, protecting regular assets and biological systems to support those on the way.

Strategies and practices that focus on economical asset the executives, biodiversity protection, and environment strength mirror a guarantee to intergenerational value. Moral chiefs gauge the drawn out results of current activities, looking for arrangements that safeguard the climate and backing the requirements of people in the future.

II. The Test of Urbanization:

1. **Metropolitan Extension and Territory Misfortune:**
   The quick extension of metropolitan regions, driven by populace development and financial turn of events, represents a huge test to protection endeavors. Urbanization prompts living space misfortune, discontinuity, and the change of normal scenes into assembled conditions. This infringement undermines biodiversity and disturbs biological systems.
   Offsetting human necessities with protection objectives in metropolitan regions requires vital metropolitan arranging that consolidates green spaces, jelly untamed life passages, and coordinates reasonable plan standards. Executing approaches that advance minimized and productive metropolitan improvement mitigates the ecological effect of urbanization.

2. **Practical Metropolitan Plan:**

   Practical metropolitan plan addresses a vital technique for orchestrating human necessities and protection objectives in metropolitan regions. This approach includes making urban communities that are versatile, asset effective, and environmentally touchy. Elements like green rooftops, metropolitan parks, and effective public transportation add to the general supportability of metropolitan conditions.

   Cooperative endeavors between metropolitan organizers, planners, policymakers, and networks are fundamental for coordinating supportable plan standards into metropolitan turn of events. Advancing blended use advancements, upgrading public transportation framework, and focusing on green structure rehearses are moral goals chasing feasible urbanization.

   III. Farming and Food Security:

1. **Concentrated Agribusiness and Ecological Effect:**
   The need to take care of a developing worldwide populace has prompted the escalation of farming, described by monoculture, weighty pesticide

use, and huge scope water system. While tending to food security, concentrated horticulture adds to soil corruption, water contamination, and biodiversity misfortune.

Offsetting human necessities with protection objectives in agribusiness includes progressing towards reasonable and regenerative practices. Agroecological approaches, natural cultivating, and accuracy farming can improve food creation while limiting the ecological effect. Supporting limited scope ranchers and advancing mindful land stewardship are vital parts of feasible food frameworks.

2. **Land Use Change and Environment Transformation:**

The transformation of normal scenes into rural land, especially for cash harvests and domesticated animals cultivating, represents a huge danger to biodiversity and biological system wellbeing. Deforestation, wetland waste, and the transformation of normal prairies add to the deficiency of basic territories and the uprooting of local species.

Moral land use rehearses in agribusiness involve executing strategies that advance feasible land use, safeguarding naturally delicate regions, and boosting agroforestry and protection well disposed cultivating techniques. Building mindfulness among ranchers and the overall population about the significance of keeping up with normal environments for long haul farming efficiency is likewise vital.

IV. Environmental Change and Variation:

1. **Modified Environments and Strength:**
Environmental change represents an imposing test to both human social orders and regular biological systems. Climbing temperatures, changing precipitation examples, and outrageous climate occasions can adjust biological systems, making them less versatile to ecological stressors. Changes in vegetation zones, disturbances to transient examples, and the spread of obtrusive species are undeniably connected to environmental change.

Offsetting human necessities with preservation objectives notwithstanding environmental change requires versatile land the board techniques. This might include reforestation endeavors, the foundation of environment versatile passages for untamed life movement, and the preservation of regular carbon sinks like woodlands and wetlands.

2. **Ocean Level Ascent and Waterfront Preservation:**

Environmental change-prompted ocean level ascent represents a critical danger to seaside biological systems and the networks that rely upon them. Beach front disintegration, saltwater interruption into freshwater frameworks, and the deficiency of important wetlands are among the results of rising ocean levels. Safeguarding beach front territories is vital for biodiversity and for buffering against the effects of outrageous climate occasions.

Moral contemplations in waterfront preservation include carrying out undertakings, for example, mangrove reforestation and the making of fake reefs to relieve the impacts of ocean level ascent. Incorporating environment transformation measures into waterfront advancement plans is fundamental to guarantee the drawn out maintainability of beach front biological systems.

V. Native Freedoms and Local area Based Preservation:

1. **Relocation and Social Effect:**

   Land use preservation endeavors frequently meet with domains customarily occupied by Native people group. Relocation coming about because of protection drives can have significant social, social, and financial effects on these networks. The deficiency of tribal terrains and interruption of conventional practices can prompt a deficiency of biodiversity information and intensify social disparities.

   Offsetting human necessities with protection objectives requires regarding and perceiving Native land privileges. Cooperative methodologies that include Native people group in dynamic cycles, consolidate customary environmental information, and backing maintainable land the executives rehearses add to both preservation objectives and the prosperity of Native people groups.

2. **Protection and Jobs:**

   Native people group frequently assume a significant part in practical land the executives and biodiversity preservation. Their customary practices, established in a profound comprehension of neighborhood environments, add to the flexibility of regular living spaces. In any case, preservation strategies that don't represent the necessities and privileges of Native people group can prompt contentions and subvert protection endeavors.

   Moral contemplations in local area based preservation drives include carrying out projects that enable Native people group, maintain their privileges, and perceive their commitments. Cooperative preservation models that incorporate customary information with logical methodologies can prompt more successful and comprehensive land use protection.

VI. Protection Money and Maintainable The travel industry:

1. **Monetary Motivations for Preservation:**

   Protection finance, including installments for environment administrations and biodiversity counterbalances, addresses an inventive way to deal with offsetting human necessities with preservation objectives. By appointing financial worth to biological system administrations, like clean water, carbon sequestration, and natural surroundings safeguarding, protection finance looks to boost landowners and networks to partake in preservation endeavors.

Moral contemplations in protection finance include guaranteeing that financial motivators line up with preservation objectives and add to the prosperity of neighborhood networks. Straightforward and responsible monetary systems, combined with impartial advantage sharing game plans, are vital for the progress of protection finance drives.

2. **Manageable The travel industry Practices:**

The travel industry, when not oversaw dependably, can add to living space debasement, social interruption, and overexploitation of normal assets. Reasonable the travel industry rehearses try to limit the adverse consequence of the travel industry while giving monetary advantages to neighborhood networks and advancing preservation mindfulness.

Moral contemplations in economical the travel industry include embracing rehearses that focus on ecological protection, regard nearby societies, and add to local area advancement. Executing conveying limit limits, advancing eco-accommodating facilities, and including nearby networks in the travel industry arranging are fundamental for accomplishing a harmony among the travel industry and preservation objectives.

VII. Training and Mindfulness:

1. **Natural Instruction:**
   Encouraging a harmony between human necessities and preservation objectives requires broad ecological training and mindfulness. Instructing general society about the significance of biodiversity, biological system administrations, and the effect of human exercises on the climate engages people to settle on informed decisions.

   Coordinating ecological training into school educational plans, leading public mindfulness missions, and utilizing computerized stages for natural correspondence add to building an all the more earth cognizant society. Informed residents are bound to help approaches and practices that focus on preservation.

2. **Public Commitment and Promotion:**

   Offsetting human requirements with preservation objectives requires dynamic public commitment and support. Residents, as partners in land use choices, assume a urgent part in holding legislatures, organizations, and protection associations responsible for moral and manageable practices.

Making roads for public investment, supporting grassroots promotion endeavors, and encouraging a culture of natural stewardship add to a more comprehensive and popularity based way to deal with land use independent direction. Educated and drawn in residents are fundamental for driving positive change at nearby, public, and worldwide levels.

10.2 Social Justice in Land Use Decision-Making

Civil rights in land use navigation perceives the significance of decency, inclusivity, and evenhanded conveyance of advantages and weights. How land is overseen and used straightforwardly influences networks, impacting admittance to assets, financial open doors, and generally speaking prosperity. This exposition investigates the standards of civil rights with regards to land use direction, accentuating the requirement for comprehensive cycles that think about the assorted necessities and viewpoints, everything being equal.

1. **Comprehensive Dynamic Cycles:**
1. **Local area Commitment:**

    Civil rights in land use dynamic starts with significant local area commitment. Nearby people group, especially those straightforwardly impacted via land use changes, ought to have the potential chance to partake in dynamic cycles. This contribution guarantees that assorted voices, including those generally underestimated, are heard and thought of.

    States, policymakers, and engineers should focus on comprehensive commitment systems, like formal reviews, local area studios, and interviews, to accumulate information and experiences from occupants. Perceiving the information and encounters of local area individuals improves the authenticity and reasonableness of land use choices.

2. **Participatory Preparation:**

    Civil rights requires a takeoff from hierarchical arranging ways to deal with participatory arranging that effectively includes networks in molding the eventual fate of their environmental elements. Through cooperative cycles, local area individuals can contribute nearby information, express their requirements, and co-make arrangements that line up with their goals.

    Participatory arranging cultivates a feeling of responsibility and strengthening inside networks, guaranteeing that land use choices mirror the needs and upsides of those straightforwardly influenced. Comprehensive arranging processes add to the making of additional reasonable and evenhanded metropolitan and rustic scenes.

    II. Impartial Admittance to Assets:

1. **Reasonable Lodging:**
   Civil rights in land use dynamic tends to lodging differences by elevating impartial admittance to reasonable lodging. Land strategies ought to focus on the advancement of reasonable lodging choices, forestalling uprooting and guaranteeing that networks with shifting pay levels can get to protected and appropriate lodging.

   In metropolitan preparation, drafting guidelines that help blended pay areas and inclusionary lodging approaches are key devices for cultivating social value. Reasonable lodging drives ought to be incorporated into more extensive land use techniques to address the intricate interaction of lodging, monetary, and civil rights.

2. **Admittance to Green Spaces:**

   Civil rights additionally includes giving impartial admittance to green spaces and sporting facilities. Parks and regular scenes add to local area prosperity, emotional wellness, and in general personal satisfaction. Land use choices ought to consider the dissemination of green spaces to guarantee that all networks, paying little heed to financial status, approach these fundamental assets.

   Metropolitan arranging that focuses on the creation and support of parks in underserved neighborhoods advances civil rights. Furthermore, endeavors ought to be made to forestall the removal of networks because of green space advancement, accentuating cooperative methodologies that regard the current social texture.

   III. Tending to Ecological Prejudice:

1. **Ecological Equity:**
   Land use choices should stand up to and amend natural prejudice - the unbalanced weight of ecological dangers on underestimated networks. Frequently, low-pay and minority networks endure the worst part of contamination, modern exercises, and perilous waste destinations. Civil rights requests that land use strategies effectively work to dispense with these inconsistencies.

   Integrating standards of ecological equity into land use direction includes leading careful natural effect appraisals, tending to aggregate effects, and keeping away from the convergence of dirtying enterprises in weak networks. Perceiving the freedoms of impacted networks to a perfect and solid climate is fundamental for advancing social value.

2. **Relieving Relocation:**

   Land use choices, especially those related with metropolitan turn of events and foundation projects, can add to relocation, lopsidedly influencing underestimated networks. Civil rights requires proactive measures to relieve dislodging, for example, reasonable lodging arrangements, local area land trusts, and approaches that focus on the maintenance of existing local area structures.

Local area driven improvement procedures and arrangements that forestall improvement support civil rights goals by guaranteeing that inhabitants are not automatically dislodged because of land use changes. Comprehensive dynamic cycles that integrate the viewpoints of impacted networks are crucial for exploring the intricacies of metropolitan improvement without worsening social imbalances.

IV. Native Privileges and Social Protection:

1. **Acknowledgment of Native Privileges:**
   Civil rights in land use direction recognizes and maintains the freedoms of Native people group to their tribal grounds. Native people groups frequently have profound social associations with the land, and their freedoms should be regarded in dynamic cycles that influence their domains. Legislatures and leaders ought to take part in significant counsel with Native people group, regarding the standards of Free, Earlier, and Informed Assent (FPIC). This includes perceiving Native administration structures, customary information, and the right to self-assurance in land use choices.

2. **Social Safeguarding:**

   Civil rights involves safeguarding and celebrating social variety, particularly despite land use choices that might compromise social legacy. Endeavors ought to be made to safeguard holy destinations, customary practices, and social scenes, perceiving their significance to the character and prosperity of Native and nearby networks.

   Cooperative methodologies that incorporate Native points of view into land use arranging, support social legacy protection drives, and guarantee fair admittance to social assets add to civil rights goals. Social awareness and responsiveness are central in accomplishing a harmony between improvement objectives and the protection of social legacy.

V. Financial Open doors and Occupation Creation:

1. **Fair Monetary Turn of events:**
   Civil rights requires land use choices that advance fair monetary turn of events, extending to open doors for employment opportunity creation and financial headway for all individuals from the local area. This includes considering the expected social and financial effects of improvement projects on various segment gatherings.

Approaches that empower the foundation of organizations in underserved regions, support nearby business, and focus on work preparing programs add to civil rights in land use navigation. Monetary improvement systems ought to address verifiable incongruities and advance comprehensive development.

2. **Local area Advantages Arrangements:**

To guarantee that neighborhood networks benefit from land use choices, civil rights requires the foundation of Local area Advantages Arrangements (CBAs). CBAs are legitimately official agreements among engineers and networks, framing explicit advantages, like reasonable lodging, open positions, or framework upgrades, that will result from an improvement project.

Integrating CBAs into land use dynamic cycles guarantees that the positive results of advancement are shared fairly among local area individuals. This approach advances straightforwardness, responsibility, and the fair dissemination of advantages and weights related with land use changes.

10.3 Ethical Dilemmas in Conservation Practices

Moral predicaments in preservation rehearses frequently emerge from the pressure between the basic to secure and save the climate and the intricacies of human connections with biological systems. These problems feature the nuanced independent direction expected to explore the moral elements of preservation endeavors.

One noticeable moral issue includes the compromise between biodiversity protection and human turn of events. Protection drives some of the time meet with regions essential for financial development, prompting clashes over land use. Finding some kind of harmony between saving normal natural surroundings and meeting the financial necessities of networks presents an ethical problem. Moral leaders should wrestle with inquiries of equity, guaranteeing that preservation endeavors don't excessively affect defenseless or underestimated populaces.

Another moral test arises in the domain of untamed life the board. Protection rehearses now and then include intercessions, for example, winnowing or movement to control creature populaces and alleviate human-natural life clashes. These actions raise moral worries in regards to the prosperity and independence of individual creatures, provoking a cautious assessment of the moral legitimizations for such mediations and the investigation of option, more empathetic methodologies.

Besides, the commitment of Native people group in preservation endeavors presents moral predicaments connected with social responsiveness and regard for conventional information. Finding some kind of harmony between the objectives of biodiversity protection and the freedoms and viewpoints of Native people groups requires exploring complex moral territory, including issues of assent, portrayal, and fair advantage sharing.

Moral difficulties in preservation rehearses feature the requirement for an all encompassing and comprehensive way to deal with direction. By coordinating different viewpoints, regarding social qualities, and taking into account the more extensive social ramifications of protection endeavors, professionals can explore these problems with a promise to both natural stewardship and moral obligation.